111 Pieces of Advice…

Straight from the Investor's Mouth

MARY LEMMER

DEDICATION

For entrepreneurs.

CONTENTS

ACKNOWLEDGMENTS

Thank you to the investors and entrepreneurs whose advice provided inspiration for this book.

Thank you to my family and friends who proofread, edited, and put up with my writing tantrums.

Thank you to beta readers for your patience and feedback.

Thank you to Jessica Greenwalt of Pixelkeet for designing the book cover.

1 INTRODUCTION

MARY LEMMER

Who Am I

I am an entrepreneur. I start and build things to create value. At age fourteen I started my first business, Iorio's (pronounced "ee-oreos"), to bring the Italian experience to my hometown in Michigan. During high school I worked on my business, catering Italian water ice at big parties, events, and other gatherings. As the catering business proved successful and customers asked for a permanent place to get their frozen dessert fix, we opened a seasonal retail store to experiment with the retail model. From there we opened a year-round retail store inside of a market, still testing out the product-market fit. Inspired by travels to Italy and recognizing the unique opportunity to share that experience with Americans, we expanded our product line, offering authentic, Italian gelato, made with local, fresh ingredients, and later expanded our retail footprint.

Starting this venture piqued my interest in entrepreneurship. After a close family friend, who happens to be a venture capitalist, suggested I attend a venture capital and entrepreneurship conference in Michigan, I signed up for the event that would be more impactful to me than I initially expected. As a graduating senior in high school, at age 17, I attended the Michigan Growth Capital Symposium, an event where over 450 investors, entrepreneurs, and other stakeholders come together to meet and find mutually beneficial opportunities. The first day of the conference I clearly stuck out like a sore thumb, because:
1. I was 17 years old and looked like I was 12 years old;
2. I was one of the few females in attendance;
3. I was wearing a pink skirt in a sea of black and grey.
I was pretty much opposite of the average attendee (Over 40 years old, male, and wearing shades of grey).

Regardless of my differences, other conference attendees were welcoming and helpful. Fearlessly, I shared my story and reasons I came to the conference, asked attendees about different terms I heard and didn't know, and asked entrepreneurs about their businesses.

The Michigan Growth Capital Symposium was my start to building relationships in the Michigan entrepreneurial and venture community. While attending the University of Michigan I got my hands on several more entrepreneurial ventures. Iorio's continued to operate while I got involved on campus, helped tech startups, worked part-time jobs, built more relationships in the entrepreneurial community, and oh yeah, took classes.

While attending the University of Michigan I worked on several ventures ranging from food distribution and organic apparel to clean tech and medical devices. During school I also started an internet company, TerraPerks, with another University of Michigan student. We learned a lot from this experience…enough to warrant its own book, or at least a blog post: http://www.venturegal.com/2012/01/17/energyflairstory

Check out www.marylemmer.com for more about my ventures.

Why I Wrote This Book

I wrote this book for you. I wrote this book for me. I wrote this book for the entrepreneur in all of us. For anyone who is starting something new in order to create value. For any entrepreneur who has ever tried to raise capital, and failed to do so, or succeeded in doing so. For any investor who has ever sat across a table from an entrepreneur inspiring these one-liners. For anyone curious about what investors really think.

For three years I had the opportunity to learn the inner workings of venture capital (VC). During this time I learned a lot and took a lot of notes. Rather than keep all this knowledge to myself, I decided to share on my blog, VentureGal.com, and more formerly in this book.

At RPM Ventures I worked directly with the partners. While working at RPM Ventures I did not call one partner, Marc Weiser, my "boss." Rather, I referred to him as my "venture coach," as I viewed him more as a mentor to learn about venture capital and building venture-backable companies. I diligently took notes from the pearls of wisdom he, and other investors I worked with, shared during board meetings, pitches, partner meetings, annual meetings, and other ripe opportunities. Rather than keep those notes to myself, sitting in a notebook or document on my computer, I decided to share what I learned with entrepreneurs, so they too can hear the wisdom itself, straight from the investor's mouth.

What to Expect

There are 111 one-liners in this book – all said straight from the mouths of investors. After each single piece of advice I elaborate on the one-liner, often sharing a story or example related to the advice. For each piece of advice I summarize the bottom line lesson for entrepreneurs. The book is split into six parts, dividing the advice by what investors have to say about **the people, the market, the model, the product, the fundraise, and the**

life.

- **The People** offers advice about hiring, culture, leadership, and entrepreneur traits.
- **The Market** advice focuses on customers, sales, and evaluating overall market opportunity.
- **The Model** dives into advice about business models and especially figuring out the viability of your model before scaling.
- **The Product** covers advice about testing, launching, and scaling products and/or services.
- **The Fundraise** includes advice about how best to tell your story to investors as well as some tips around structuring a deal with investors.
- **The Life** shares advice about living the startup life and the life of investors.

About Marc Weiser and RPM Ventures

Marc Weiser, an entrepreneur and VC since 1992, is the Founder and Managing Director of RPM Ventures, a seed and early stage venture capital firm based in Ann Arbor, Michigan. Prior to forming RPM Ventures, Marc was an entrepreneur in the internet and software space. He co-founded QuantumShift, a provider of web-based business-to-business technology and services focused on corporate telecommunications needs. He was also an early employee at MessageMedia (acquired by DoubleClick) where he pioneered some of the original methods for e-commerce and helped lead the company's IPO. To learn more about Marc or RPM Ventures, visit www.rpmvc.com.

---

2 THE PEOPLE

The People section offers advice covering hiring, culture, leadership, and entrepreneur traits. People are the most important part of every organization, making it critical, as an entrepreneur, to treat them as such.

MARY LEMMER

1. **People love the idea of being a part of building something.**

It's human nature. People like to be a part of something bigger than themselves - working toward a big mission to make a positive impact in the world. Everyone has different levels of drive, but ultimately, if you create an environment where people feel a part of building something, your team will thrive.

Lesson for entrepreneurs:

Be transparent and inclusive with your team. It will bolster motivation and everyone working toward a common goal.

2. **Best cultures are deliberately designed and not something you fall into.**

An entire book could be written about this point, as building and sustaining culture are imperative in company's growth. If you don't choose culture, the culture will choose you. Okay, not exactly, but if you aren't deliberate about creating your culture, a culture will emerge, and that emerging culture may or may not be the culture you want for your company.

With so many pulls in different directions – from product, marketing, fundraising, and so forth – culture may get the short end of the stick or fall off the priority list very easily. Don't let it. Make time for culture. Ultimately, it will be more important than all the other forces pulling at you.

There are three key things that need to be done to embed culture in an organization:

1. *Define it.* Write it down. Share it with everyone. It may be clear in your head but that doesn't mean it's clear to everyone else. Write down your mission, vision, and values, so it's concrete and easily sharable with your team.

2. *Live it.* It's hard to create a thriving culture in an organization if you don't spend time living the culture. Practice what you preach and be the best example of the culture in your organization. Really, how do you expect to embed a culture where you don't fit? Living the culture means taking time to spend with your team,

demonstrating your commitment to the culture through both promising and challenging times.

3. ***Measure it.*** You can't track what you don't measure, so how do you expect to track whether your culture is flowing through the organization if you don't measure it? How do you measure it? With enough people you may do employee surveys. It also could be a key metric on a dashboard that is tracked regularly. You can also test it with congruency – how well does your team align with the company culture? One of the best examples I have of measuring culture is an anecdote from my own business, Iorio's. At Iorio's, our team thrives because of our culture…it's open, it's fun, it's consistent, and it's clear. Since we have a fun, open culture, we want to make sure we're creating a great employee experience. Our dashboard includes a "Sweet Life" score, for which we ask one team member, on a scale of 1 to 10 (1 being as sour as a Sour Patch Kid and 10 as the ultimate sweet), how sweet her/his week was working at Iorio's. When someone responds less than 10, we ask "What would have made it a 10?" so to constantly keep track of how we can create a better work experience for our team members. In addition to measuring culture using quantitative metrics, there are also subtle or qualitative clues that the culture is aligned. I about shed a tear when someone on the team handed over "Iorio's Commandments" he wrote which embodied our culture to a tee. Our team gets it. It's alive. It's real because we define it, live it, and measure it regularly.

Lesson for entrepreneurs:

Be a culture snob. Be deliberate about the culture you are building at your company. If you're not, find a business partner who is. It's really important for building a team and environment to scale. Define it. Live it. Measure it.

3. **The difference between a corporate employee and an employee in a startup company is that a corporate employee is more concerned with her/his career, and a startup employee is more concerned with the success of the company.**

There are three factors that drive this distinction:

1. ***Selection bias.*** People who choose to work for startups tend to

be more entrepreneurial, have a higher tolerance for risk, and are chasing dreams of making a huge impact with huge reward.

People working for big companies tend to be more risk averse and less entrepreneurially driven. This is not a hard and fast rule – just in general.

2. **Path to the top.** At a startup, promotion is aligned with accomplishments and output, regardless of age, past experience, or future career path. Within months or even weeks at a startup, an employee may find her/himself promoted to, or just changed to, a different role – a time horizon that is almost unheard of at larger, more established companies.

At larger corporations there are often career ladders built up and processes set in place for getting promoted and rising to the top. Promotion at larger companies takes building a career, either specifically at that company, or within a specific function. Scaling the corporate career ladder takes time and requires following the right steps.

3. **Options.** In many cases, employees at a startup receive a large portion of their compensation in the form of options. They have an interest in the company's success; the better the company does, the better their compensation will be (the higher the value of the options).

At large companies, employees, too, receive stock, but the percentage of the entire compensation represented by stock is not nearly as much as typical for a startup.

Lesson for entrepreneurs:

When hiring, especially early employees, keep in mind these differences and define for yourself what is most important to you and your company. High achievers are great, but consider whether you want someone who is a personal career builder or someone who is going to put the company ahead of personal satisfaction. Build into your interview process questions and exercises to test candidates' primary interests, so to find people who best align with your interests.

4. Nothing brings a team together like a common enemy.

Many friendships and relationships are spawned from mutual interests. You meet someone at an art class, bond over watercolor, and develop a beautiful friendship. After all, shared interests, whether reflecting positive or negative energy, can bring people together.

So it should be no surprise that commonalities among your team can bring your team closer together. Even if that commonality is a common enemy. Who is your company's biggest competitor? Is everyone in the company aware of this competitor? Can your team bond over the desire to beat the competition? Certainly, if you want to make that a point to bond over. Of course, there are other, more positive energy ways to bring your team together. For example, your shared vision for changing the world with your company, or shared love for foosball. Whatever it is, know that commonalities add a "We" to "Team!"

Lesson for entrepreneurs:

Love your friends and respect your enemies. They may both be helpful for different reasons.

5. Investors believe you can do that which you've done in the past.

Curious why entrepreneurs who previously built and sold companies can raise money with their eyes closed? Well, maybe not with eyes closed, but seemingly easier than first-time entrepreneurs. This piece of wisdom sums it all up. Investors are great at pattern recognition. Entrepreneurs building and selling companies in the past is a pattern investors recognize as being repeatable. A previously successful entrepreneur de-risks the deal for investors because they believe the chances for success are higher if the entrepreneur has been through the process before. Data shows that successful entrepreneurs who previously started a company demonstrate the entrepreneurial DNA that is imperative to building a valuable company.

Lesson for entrepreneurs:

When sharing your story with investors make sure to mention your previous successes, whether building large audiences online, increasing sales, and/or building and selling a company. Highlight your proudest moments. Also be honest about the times you fell on your face. Be authentic about your strengths and weaknesses, your high and low points. Share what you learned from challenges and you'll come out victorious, as investors trust people who have failed and learned (more so than people who mask mistakes).

6.   Anybody who is talented is not available.

The most talented people already have jobs. That means to get the best talent you will likely need to poach people from other companies. To hire any talented person, especially if hiring someone from another job, you need to be convincing. The best entrepreneurs are incredible at attracting talent and convincing talented people to leave current opportunities to join their company.

Lesson for entrepreneurs:

Looking for fresh blood? To find top talent, don't limit yourself to unemployed people actively looking for jobs. Search for people who already have jobs. The best people are more likely to already be at another company and it is up to you to find them and convince them to join you. A good place to start, when looking for that right person, is to look at comparable positions at similar types of companies. For instance, if you are an online marketplace looking for a front-end developer, look for front-end developers at other online marketplaces. LinkedIn can be a useful tool for this research, as well as asking people within your network for personal referrals.

7.   You can tell people, but sometimes you need to show people.

People learn differently. You probably heard that there are different types of learners in the world: some learn by listening, others by seeing, and most through actually doing. Considering some people are visual learners, some learn by listening, and others by doing, teaching people isn't as clear-cut as handing over a manual. Sometimes telling people is enough, but more often you need to show people in order for them to truly understand.

It's not just employees you'll need to train, but also customers or partners. For instance, one startup company our investment firm investigated was selling an online service to automotive dealers, and to ensure the dealers used the service the startup company created an in-person training that was engaging, interactive, and helpful in teaching the dealers how best to use the service to improve their dealerships (and ultimately improve sales for the startup company as well). A manual, though informative, probably wouldn't have the same impact in teaching and engraining the principals and usefulness of the service. Not all products/services will necessarily require an in-person training (or any training at all), but keep in mind that using your product/service probably isn't as intuitive to others as it is to you.

Lesson for entrepreneurs:

Be aware of learning types when training people, working with customers, and when engaged in other interactions. Use multiple teaching methods to ensure people understand and remember to explain why and how to do something. Especially when you are training new team members and customers, it is important to show people what to do, or how to do something, and the benefit of those actions. It may take more time upfront, but in the long run it will save you time and headaches.

8. If you're a dabbler, you're never successful.

Focus your efforts. Dabbling in multiple projects means you're not putting 200% effort into a single venture. Early stage companies require lots of effort. Successful companies are built by entrepreneurs working max effort on a single venture.

Another reason dabblers aren't successful – if you are scattering your efforts, hedging your bets effectively, you have less incentive to make any one work. Because if one doesn't work out, you still have others to fall back on. This "portfolio" approach to ventures reduces commitment to success of any single venture and it's this lack of commitment that will demonstrate itself when none of the ventures end up wildly successful.

That being said, success is all in how you define it. The requirements to building a billion dollar company and building a self-sustaining lifestyle business are different, and it is entirely possible to build a self-sustaining lifestyle business and keep it operating while re-focusing your time on a new venture. At any given time though your focus will predominantly be on one.

For venture-backable, high growth companies, it's a red flag to investors when they see dabbling entrepreneurs. If you're running multiple companies, organizing Meetup groups, participating on several nonprofit boards, acting as the president of various clubs, and running a company, be prepared to address your commitment to the venture for which you're raising capital. That being said, some of the most successful CEOs I have met are some of the best time managers. You have to be, especially if you want to a) keep your sanity, and b) have a life beyond work. Investors really want to see commitment, and by spreading yourself too thin, you risk scaring investors from your seemingly lack of commitment to your venture. Show commitment in your actions and by delivering results.

Lesson for entrepreneurs:

Commit.

9. A weakness is a strength if you know it's a weakness.

Recognizing weaknesses is knowledge. Knowledge is power. Once you build self-awareness to recognize your weaknesses, you can understand how best to allocate your time and resources.

Lesson for entrepreneurs:

Spend time with yourself. Learn about yourself. Develop mentors and ask them to be honest about your strengths and weaknesses. Be honest about your own strengths and weaknesses. When you know your shortcomings you can better hire people to complement your weaknesses.

10. Contractors ease you through the gates of hell. I've never seen a successful company built with all contractors.

Part of building value in your company involves you actually building it! When you outsource the work required to build your company you are outsourcing part of what will create value for your company.

Contracting work also puts the control in the hands of the contractor, in many ways. If you are hiring someone else to do the work, you don't always own the process, nor can you always get work done at the speed at which is often required or desired.

Also, by hiring someone to work directly for you, you demonstrate your ability to attract and recruit talent, one of the most important skills of entrepreneurs.

There's a caveat to this advice – hiring contractors can be great for testing people out before hiring them full time. "Try before you buy" doesn't only apply to test-driving cars!

Lesson for entrepreneurs:

Build in-house when possible. Not only does it demonstrate that you can attract and recruit talent, it also creates more value for your company.

11. There is no good or bad culture...just the culture you want to build.

Every company has a culture. What that culture is and the strength of it will depend on the leadership team's thoughtfulness in defining and executing the culture.

Take these two examples of culture:

Company A has a flexible, laid back culture, in which employees roll in around 10 a.m., dressed in casual garb and ready to work between snacking on free food available at the office and petting coworkers' dogs. The collaboration between employees resembles college friends and there are commonly mid-afternoon breaks to play video games or sleep in a nap pod.

Company B employees show up to the office anywhere from 6:30 am until 10 am, depending on the team they're on and what is happening that day. The attire ranges from shorts and a t-shirt to full out dress slacks and tie. There are a few snacks available. The relationship between employees more closely resembles the stereotypical coworker relationships – friendly, but limited, and more formal than casual.

Which Company would you prefer to join (or start)? There is no right or wrong answer, and neither of these cultures is "better" than the other. Some folks at Company A may consider Company B's culture to be inferior, and vice versa, but truth is...there is no right or wrong culture, but there is culture. The more deliberate you are about designing your culture, the better, because the culture will then closely align with you and your company values, be apparent to others so to make hiring decisions clearer, and ultimately help with scaling and retaining your team.

Lesson for entrepreneurs:

Consider culture! Build a culture you want to enjoy and that will attract others you'd like to work with you. There is no perfect culture, nor are there good and bad cultures. Rather, there is the culture **YOU** design, so be deliberate in designing your culture!

12. Somebody who wants to work in a startup already knows it.

You know you want to be an entrepreneur if you have aspirations of starting a company or working for a startup, and doing nothing else sounds right to you. Being an entrepreneur isn't something you choose. It chooses you.

This piece of advice came up during one of our weekly partners meetings. We were discussing young talent and the folks we encountered debating whether or not to start a company or join a startup, versus accepting a job offer from a larger corporation. The opinions were unanimous: if there's any question, a startup life is probably not for you.

This topic also came up during a lecture led by Brad Keywell, the founder of Groupon. Brad is a graduate of the University of Michigan and clearly has entrepreneurial DNA. Someone asked Brad about how to know whether or not to start a company. Brad responded by letting the student know that you just know, and if there's even a question in your mind, don't start a company.

Lesson for entrepreneurs:

Be honest with yourself. Why are you starting a company or working for a startup? What are your motivations? Do you have what it takes? How do (or will) you react when things get tough? When will you quit? Answering these questions will help determine whether or not you are "called" to be an entrepreneur. Because ultimately, being an entrepreneur isn't something you choose. It chooses you.

13. There is an art of not letting someone say "no" if they're not going to say "yes."

Some people are better at this than others and it's a great skill for entrepreneurs to build. Think back to your last negotiation or discussion with a potential business partner or investor…a discussion that ended with the business partner or investor saying "no." Could you have deterred the "no" response, even though it may have seemed clear that "yes" was not going to be the answer? By not letting someone say "no" even if they're not going to say "yes" you keep the door open for the conversation to continue. You leave space for the possibility that the potential business partner or investor's mind will change and the answer will be "yes."

These are some tips for turning an eminent "no" to a "maybe," delayed "yes," or just a prolonged "no:"

- Ask questions such as "What do you need to see/know in order to make a decision?"
- Recommend "Keeping the dialogue open" to discuss any remaining questions, ideas, etc.
- Come with a backup point – some milestone, big event or significant news you are anticipating in the near future. Bringing this point up will inevitably make the investor wait to hear the results from the event/news/etc. It can, however, put more time on your clock to sway an unspoken "no" to a possible "yes."
- Schedule a follow up conversation before leaving the meeting. In between your initial meeting and the follow up meeting, spend time addressing the other party's main points of concern or criticism (some which will not be so easily changed, like industry, your lack of experience) and preparing to address mitigation in the follow up messages.

On the flipside, VCs can be notorious for not saying "no" or "yes," but rather keeping entrepreneurs on the edge of their seat, with hope that the long subdued silence will eventually transpire to a "yes." **Usually, no news is not good news.** If an investor does not stay in touch with you it's probably because there's no interest. It's similar to dating. If a guy wants to see you, he will see you (great wisdom shared in the movie "He's Just Not That Into You"). If an investor wants to stay in touch, she/he will stay in touch.

Lesson for entrepreneurs:

If you sense a "no" coming on, and you want a "yes," try some techniques to not let someone say "no." Or, if you lack patience and want a firm "yes" or "no" immediately, be careful how you spin the conversation. When left to their own devices investors may not give you either even when the decision has been made up in their mind.

14. Don't put your destiny in the hands of other people.

When someone, besides you, owns your destiny, the outcome is far more outside of your control. When you give control of your destiny to someone else, you're on a path likely to lead to disappointment. Take ownership of your destiny. Put yourself in control of your outcomes. If your work effort is more or less correlated with your rewards, you'll be more motivated and satisfied.

Here are some examples of putting your destiny in the hands of other people, in an entrepreneurial context:

- Depending on a partnership to come through, in order to convince investors to invest, to generate revenue, or to make a new hire.
- Relying on a handful of customers for the majority of your revenue.
- Depending on accounts receivable to be paid, in order to make payroll.
- Waiting on investors (for anything).

Don't fall into the trap of giving anyone else too much power over your destiny. Waiting on a big partnership to close? Great! Have other irons in the fire and don't put all your weight on that one partnership. Don't bet the farm as the saying goes. Be prepared so that if something doesn't happen as you intend, you're not shutting down your business because of it.

Lesson for entrepreneurs:

Take ownership of your destiny. Be your own leader. Of course, find people to help along the way, but never let go of all the reins.

15. Sometimes your best VP of Sales is someone from Sales Operations.

Great salespeople don't necessarily make great sales managers. One of our portfolio companies once promoted a great salesperson to be a sales manager, and unfortunately, he didn't cut it as a great sales manager. Just because someone is great at selling widgets doesn't mean she/he is great at managing a team of people selling widgets.

A strong VP of Sales holds salespeople accountable and holds their feet to the metrics. Since sales operations tends to focus on metrics – looking at sales cycle time, cost per customer acquisition, and other data that informs improvements to the sales team – a likely great candidate for a VP of Sales role is someone with a sales operations background.

A strong VP of Sales will be someone who pays close attention to metrics. A strong VP of Sales measures all sales people to trackable metrics. A strong VP of sales needs to give salespeople the tools to help them be successful and if they aren't successful the VP needs to be disciplined with making the appropriate improvements, even if that means cutting people or shifting territories.

Lesson for entrepreneurs:

When considering whom to make your VP of Sales, look for a sales operations background in addition to (or instead of) simply sales experience. Finding someone who is metrics-driven and disciplined with execution will help your company tremendously as you build out and scale your sales' efforts.

16. Everyone has his or her own personal obsessive-compulsive disorder (OCD) and it's important to honor it.

Great entrepreneurs are detail-oriented and sometimes a bit obsessive. Entrepreneurs are driven, habitual, high achievers. Recognize what your OCD behavior is and feel no shame. It may be as common as washing your hands obsessively and not touching door knobs, to avoid germs and getting sick. I know CEOs who are compulsive about going for a run every day. Or the habit could be as eccentric as drinking purple Kool-Aid every day at 1 p.m. The latter behavior is probably not as great for your health, but if that's what keeps you in check do it.

Lesson for entrepreneurs:

Be yourself. Recognize your quirks, however strange you or others may think they are, and own them. Sometimes these seemingly odd behaviors are what get you through challenging and stressful times.

17. Entrepreneurs use capital they have to prove they deserve more. Wantrepreneurs complain they don't have enough capital.

Entrepreneurs are executors, resource allocators, and just pure drivers. Entrepreneurs take what they have and make it work to get to the next milestone. They recognize when they need to raise capital, and even though they could always use more money, they don't complain about not having money. Time complaining is better spent on building the business, so that value can be created.

Lesson for entrepreneurs:

Consider how you spend your money and more importantly, how you spend your time. The results you achieve with the capital you raise will impact your ability to build your business and raise additional capital.

Wantrepreneur (noun) An individual who aspires to be an entrepreneur, but hasn't yet done anything to warrant such a label.

---

18. **Entrepreneurs know they have things to figure out and have a framework to do so. Wantrepreneurs think they have it figured out.**

Entrepreneurs see early stage companies as experiments, continuously testing hypotheses to figure out the best decisions to make. Rarely will you hear an entrepreneur say "I think" unless it is followed by explanation of how the thought will be validated.

Lesson for entrepreneurs:

Know what you know. Know what you don't know. Don't pretend to know what you don't know. There are always questions to answer and things to learn. Don't settle for thinking you have it all figured out. It sends a signal of naiveté and inexperience.

19. **Entrepreneurs understand that there is little correlation between intellect and achievement. Desire and work ethic matter more.**

The smartest person in the room may not end up the most successful. Related to the fact that ideas are worthless and execution is everything, being smart is great, but has little to do with accomplishment. If brilliant people (as measured by IQ tests) don't put any effort into their work, life will catch up with them and ultimately they will stop achieving from pure intellect.

Consider this analogy to sports. Some people are naturally gifted. They come out of the womb tall, strong and with quick reflexes and six-pack abs. Throughout their early life, from grade school through high school, they probably don't need to work as hard as other athletes because of the natural characteristics they have in their favor. They start on the basketball court because they're tall or fast, even if they don't always show up to practice on time (or at all). On the other end of the spectrum, there are the players who are not as naturally gifted, but they work their butts off. These players develop a work ethic and drive that far exceeds the players who need not work as hard to achieve. Eventually natural ability wanes in the face of hard working competition and aging muscles and minds. Then those naturally gifted players are left with big feet and little work ethic skills or process to achieve anything in life.

Lesson for entrepreneurs:

Develop a strong work ethic because it's not only your brain or shoe size that will make you successful. Rather, it's the size of your drive and persistence.

20. There's no perfect CEO. You just have to be yourself.

Isn't that the truth for life too? There's no perfect [insert your title here]. Just be you. We learn countless times to "be ourselves" and typically when we try to be something we aren't we fall flat on our faces, as a reminder to be ourselves. It's especially true for entrepreneurs. The entrepreneurs I have seen struggle the most are the ones who chase after every suggestion to change, to the point they are running down a path further and further from themselves and their business vision.

Lesson for entrepreneurs:

Be yourself. Maybe if you hear/see it enough times you'll actually start to believe its importance for your entrepreneurial ventures and life.

21. You want to enter just as well as you exit.

With any job you want to leave as gracefully as you entered. No burning bridges, leaving items hanging, or causing a ruckus on your way out. Similarly, enter and exit a relationship with an investor with class. Respond to emails, answer your phone (and call people back), and be respectful of investors' time and input (even if you don't care for it). When an investor says "no" (because they will), don't badmouth her/him. One "no" isn't "no" forever.

Think of relationships with investors like personal relationships. Not that there's any good way to end a relationship, but there are better ways than others. The most painful end to relationships can spur feasting on pints of ice cream and listening to emo music. Don't let your investor relationships end that way.

Lesson for entrepreneurs:

Exit gracefully at the right time. The investor/entrepreneur orbit is small. There are few bridges, so don't break them.

22.   Once you hire, they are like cows.

Employees are like cows. Once you hire someone they stand in the field and keep eating the grass. Even if they aren't giving you milk.

This saying is meant to illustrate what can happen with a team. In early stage teams, value is incredibly important. If someone you hired isn't producing value, but she/he is still requiring company resources (time, training, money, benefits and perks) then you are experiencing a grazing cow that isn't producing milk. In other words, though that person is using your resources, she/he is not creating value at least equivalent to the resources she/he is taking.

Lesson for entrepreneurs:

Consider, how are you going to keep your team motivated? How will you measure value? What will you do if you notice that one of your cows isn't producing enough milk? It's likely to happen, so be prepared, or at least don't be surprised when the milk runs dry. Think about how you will motivate your team, especially early on when you may not be able to afford luxurious perks and expensive bonuses.

23.   The second you stop honoring yourself as CEO is the second

you fail as a leader.

Investors will challenge your thinking, which is good. However, when you let others influence your decision making and influence your vision too much you are setting yourself up for a downward spiral.

If you waver too much when you receive feedback from others you'll lose others' confidence in your leadership abilities. Be confident in yourself and you'll evoke a sense of confidence in your ability to lead. This advice relates back to being yourself...the most successful entrepreneurs are themselves.

Lesson for entrepreneurs:

Thoughtfully approach how to incorporate advice from investors and others. You're still CEO and are running the ship. Don't let too many people steer you or you'll just end up lost at sea.

24. Investors don't invest in part-time entrepreneurs.

Repeatedly when entrepreneurs pitched their businesses and the investors asked about commitment, the entrepreneurs stated that they would be "full time on their venture as soon as they raise capital." Until raising capital, they were moonlighting...working only on their entrepreneurial venture during nights and weekends. Certainly it's understandable that people need to pay the bills and a startup venture doesn't always have money to pay immediately. But how do you expect an investor to take a risk in investing in your business if you aren't even willing to take the risk in your venture?

Lesson for entrepreneurs:

Commit. Take a risk and maybe you'll be able to convince an investor to take a risk as well. Either you're fully in, or you're out.

25. Don't give away big titles too soon.

If you bring in an early hire and give that person a C-level title (e.g. COO), what happens when the company outgrows that person's skills and you need to bring in a more experienced COO? Are you going to demote the original COO to VP of Operations? That's a tough move and will likely leave a bad taste in your team's mouth, if not drive people away altogether.

Lesson for entrepreneurs:

Better to start people out with smaller titles and grant larger titles as earned and demonstrated that the person can handle the responsibilities associated with the big title. Plus, those quick and little promotions inspire your team to work harder and commit more to the company.

26. You can always give someone more equity later on, but once you give it you cannot get it back.

In a similar vein to assigning titles, remember that it's better to add more than it is to take away. Start someone out with less equity and let her/him earn more by demonstrating her/his abilities and value add to the company.

Lesson for entrepreneurs:

Start small and award more based on performance because once you give it, it's very hard to get back.

27. Successful failure. Every entrepreneur needs to have one.

One of my life mantras is "there are no mistakes, only gifts." It's a saying I learned studying improv and one that continues to percolate throughout my life. With investors, some investors don't trust entrepreneurs who haven't failed at something. We learn more from what doesn't go right, than from what does go right.

For instance, it's easy for an entrepreneur to look back at a company she/he built and say "well, we could've done better with online marketing, but we ended up selling to Amazon for hundreds of millions of dollars, so I guess things turned out alright" because when the outcome is favorable all that happened in the past can be justified by the favorable outcome. However, when the favorable outcome doesn't happen, it's easy to be hyper critical on what didn't go so well and glean lessons from those experiences.

Lesson for entrepreneurs:

Be fearless. Reflect on and learn from what doesn't happen as you plan or hope. You'll become a better entrepreneur and a better person.

28. When the Chief Financial Officer (CFO) starts talking about Generally Accepted Accounting Principles (GAAP), you know you have the wrong person.

In early stage companies, especially SaaS businesses, metrics, not financial statements, are key. A lot of times there is no revenue to book, just expenses and a load of performance data. Though key performance indicators aren't required to report according to GAAP, they are extremely important to the health of your business. Examples of metrics to track include cost of customer acquisition (COCA)/customer acquisition cost (CAC), churn rate, and monthly recurring revenue (MRR).

Lesson for entrepreneurs:

Hire a CFO, VP of Finance, or other financial person who understands metrics for early stage and quickly growing companies. Once you go public you can worry about GAAP reporting. If you're not sure if you need a full-time CFO, check out hiring a part-time CFO for hire, to help with your financial reporting. A part-time CFO help enables you to save some resources to hire someone to own data and metrics as you scale your business.

29. A dog with two owners dies of hunger.

Entrepreneurs with multiple owners will starve, just like dogs with multiple owners die of hunger. With dogs, the two owners assume the other feeds the dog, so that no one ends up actually feeding the dog. With entrepreneurs, for instance, entrepreneurs moonlighting, serving two owners (day job and evening project) will not be able to sustain the pace and velocity required to build a venture-backed company. Growing a company backed by investors takes significant time and energy, leaving little left in the bank for taking on multiple entrepreneurial ventures.

Similarly, a company with two equal owners will die. When two people have decision-making veto, less is likely to get done because two people have to agree before moving forward. Consider this wisdom when deciding how to allocate ownership amongst co-founders. A 50/50 split may seem most equitable at the beginning, but down the road can lead to trouble. It's not impossible, especially if appropriate agreements and processes are in place.

Lesson for entrepreneurs:

Best to keep it simple. When multiple co-founders are involved at the early stages of a company, carefully consider the ownership structure and document a decision-making process. Before investors are secured and a formal board is in place, figure out a decision-making process and put it in writing.

30. If you're doing it right, you should be spending half your time recruiting/building your team.

A CEO has a lot of responsibilities, including fundraising, setting and leading toward the company's vision, and hiring great people to help execute. The better processes and systems that are created, the less time the CEO should have to spend on activities like coordinating meetings, approving minor decisions, or sitting in non-value add meetings. For instance, if a CEO hires great people and empowers them to make decisions, she/he frees up some time that can be spent hiring more great people to continue to build out the team and expand her/his bandwidth, enabling the company to accomplish even more.

Lesson for entrepreneurs:

People are important. Spend time building relationships with and recruiting top talent. Great product and business model is one thing, but without the right people to execute you are severely limiting your potential. Spend time recruiting and building your team. You won't regret it.

3 THE MARKET

The Market section includes advice that focuses on customers, sales, and evaluating overall market opportunity. Investors look for huge market opportunities that are well understood by the entrepreneurs addressing them.

MARY LEMMER

31. The best businesses tend to follow the money.

Just like Rod Tidwell (played by Cuba Gooding Jr.) in the movie *Jerry Maguire*, always said, "show me the money." You're more likely to see the money if you are actually following the money.

What does it mean for entrepreneurs to "follow money?" It means choose big markets where customers actually pay for stuff. It means figure out what folks are paying for in order to currently solve the problem you're solving.

Following the money is the best way to get paid. Money talks. When individuals, companies, or industries are putting money to work to solve problems that is a great sign that they actually care about the problems.

Lesson for entrepreneurs:

Solve problems that money is already being spent to solve. Follow the money – find big markets, big spending, and go for it!

32. Any market under $1 billion is not interesting.

Venture capital investors invest in big market opportunities. Anything less than $1 billion is a small market opportunity. That doesn't mean it's a bad business idea or opportunity. It just isn't venture-backable. Venture capitalists need to generate significant returns and tackling big markets offers potential to build a big enough company to lead to a big exit or IPO. Trillion dollar market opportunities, even better!

Lesson for entrepreneurs:

Size your market. Do a bottoms-up and top-down analysis. To understand bottoms-up market sizing, build the microeconomics up to find out what the total market size is; and to understand top-down, look at the total market size and figure your chunk of the pie depending on what chunk of that you capture. If your total market size is less than $1 billion then venture capital may not be the best capital for you.

33. The best entrepreneurs are the ones who know their customers better than they know themselves.

This piece of advice has come straight from investors' mouths more than any other piece of advice. The advice applies to every company that tried to raise capital from our firm, every company in which we made an investment, and generally any company we discussed or evaluated (regardless of whether or not we were interested in investing). The advice is sector agnostic and stage agnostic.

What does it mean to know customers better than the customers know themselves? To know customers, entrepreneurs know things like...

- How much money customers spend on similar products/services.
- How customers measure success.
- Who is the purchase decision maker in the organization/household.

Why do entrepreneurs know their customers better than the customers know themselves? How?

- Customer discovery (more about customer discovery in advice #41).
- Experience as the customer (the entrepreneur is solving a problem she/he faced and would pay for a solution).
- Spending time learning about the customer.
- Use of data to learn things about the customer that the customer doesn't even know.

For example, one company I conducted diligence on spent time sitting in auto dealerships, observing, asking questions, and taking notes. Why? Because the entrepreneur was working on solving some inefficiencies in the way auto dealers conduct business and he truly wanted to understand how the dealerships worked so that he could put together a very compelling product/service to solve those problems.

What are the signs that a company knows the customers better than the customers know themselves? A company can demonstrate its knowledge of customers in its pitch and conversations with investors:

- Focus not only on the top-down market. Include bottoms-up analysis to demonstrate an understanding of the unit economics for customers.

- Tell stories about customers you know and have spoken to about their pain points.

- Mention your process for learning about customers. What did you do? How did you do it? And most importantly, what did you learn?

- If you've spent anytime working in the industry or as your customer, bring that up.

Here is an example of a startup that knows its customers better than they know themselves:

Paul Nadjarian, Founder and CEO of Mojo Motors.   Full disclosure, my previous firm, RPM Ventures, invested in Mojo Motors.

Paul Nadjarian is the Founder and CEO of Mojo Motors, an online automotive marketplace that helps car shoppers "Follow" cars they like, to get alerts when dealers drop prices and similar cars become available. The website is free to car shoppers, and car dealers pay a monthly marketing fee. Prior to starting Mojo Motors Paul spent extensive time in both the auto industry and online marketplaces. He started his career at Ford Motor company selling inventory and programs to auto dealers and eventually ran the internet lead management group at Ford. After Ford, Paul joined eBay Motors to run the Parts and Accessories category, growing the business to be the largest category at eBay. After eBay Paul was the head of Product and Marketing at OnForce, an online marketplace for local contract professionals. Paul has also been on the founding team of GreenLeaf Auto, an auto-recycling venture within Ford, and CombineNet, an advance sourcing and optimization platform. By the time Paul started Mojo Motors he had already spent about 10 years learning about automotive and online marketplaces. For him to build an online automotive marketplace made a lot of sense. He knows the customer. He worked with the customer for years. And it's not just the time Paul spent working in the industry that makes him an expert on his customer. It's the amount of data he understands about his business as well. For instance, Paul can tell you how much money, on average, car dealers spend on advertising. He can tell you where they spend it and who in the dealership is making the purchase decision. Why does that matter? Because the car dealership is Paul's customer and the better he understands his customer the better he will be able to find his buyers and create a value proposition for them.

Lesson for entrepreneurs:

Know your customer. Investors will know if you don't. Knowing your customer will help you raise capital and build your business.

34. Focus on one market opportunity.

Too many will distract you. That being said, be educated and aware of other potential adjacent market opportunities. Understand the overall market potential, but do not lose sight of your go-to-market strategy and the market you are prioritizing.

Lesson for entrepreneurs:

Focus on the initial market you are tackling. Don't spread yourself so thin that you are trying to tackle too many markets simultaneously. You'll likely run out of resources quickly without achieving significant tangible milestones.

35. It's great when you build something and you are the customer.

...Because then you know the customer. And as you've already learned from #33, knowing customers better than they know themselves is a key trait of great entrepreneurs.

When you solve your own problems you'll likely cure the same pain for many others. There are a lot of problems out there and a lot of people encounter the same ones. For example, Everly co-founders, Kyle McCollom and Chris Cole, created a healthier alternative to an on-the-go energizing beverage mix, after experiencing the pain during their adventures.

From their website:

Kyle's journey took him to Boundary Waters, Minnesota. He was on a weeklong canoe trip, munching on Clif Bars and using powder packets to flavor the water he filtered into his bottle. Kyle noticed that the drink mixes he had with him were chock-full of artificial ingredients, tasted like chalk, and lacked the vitamins and electrolytes he needed for the adventure. The light bulb went off in his head, and he had an idea – make a drink mix with the best natural ingredients that could be a companion product to Clif Bar.

Chris's journey took him to a clinic in Southern Bangladesh. He spent a summer learning about the harmful, often deadly, effects of dehydration, especially in conjunction with waterborne diseases among children. It impacted him greatly, and he started to think of ways he could promote healthy hydration to help others in the future.

The two ideas came together one night in the summer after Kyle and Chris graduated. As previous business partners and fledgling entrepreneurs, the synergy struck them. They set out to design a better drink mix and build a company that uses hydration to help the world. Everly was born.

Lesson for entrepreneurs:

If you have experienced the problem your company is solving, incorporate that experience into your story. Your story becomes more compelling when you're in it. Let your passion light through when you're solving a problem that deeply impacts you.

36. You have to go out there and talk to folks.

Related to #33, know your customers better than they know themselves, one of the best ways to get to know your customers is to talk to them. The amount of learning from talking to people is unprecedented. Surveys are not a suitable substitute. Get out of your building and talk to potential customers, current customers, and people you wouldn't necessarily expect to be customers. And it's not just talking to folks. It's listening. Ask questions. Listen. Then reflect on what you heard and make decisions based on what you learn.

Lesson for entrepreneurs:

Get out of your office. Go talk to people. Talk to people on buses, in elevators, at farmers markets, and anywhere else. You can only learn so much brainstorming with your own team. Talking to customers and other stakeholders will provide new perspective and inspire creative thinking about your product/services and strategy.

37. Any attractive market has competition.

I learned the "investor eye roll" quickly with this piece of wisdom. Whenever an entrepreneur claimed "we have no competition," either investors thought of an eye roll or actual eye roll ensued. Why? Because **there is always competition.** The status quo is competition. Think about it – there are plenty of reasons companies may not be addressing the same problem – one of them being that the market is unattractive. State the status quo as competition. If you think you don't have competition, investors will question how well you actually know your industry or whether the market opportunity is attractive.

Lesson for entrepreneurs:

Really figure out – what are people doing to solve the problem today? It will strengthen your pitch and understanding of your market. Avoid using the phrase "we have no competition" or "no one else is doing this" when telling investors your story. There is always competition. It may just not be as obvious as you might imagine. For example, I regularly received proposals from companies aspiring to create flying cars. And there was always "no competition." "No one else" was making and selling flying cars. That may be true. There may be no other companies making and selling flying cars. Such claims inspire investors to think a couple things:

1. If no other company is making or selling flying cars, why not? Is it not an attractive business opportunity?

2. There may not be other companies making and selling flying cars, but there is competition. The status quo is competition. Regular cars are competition. Heck, bicycle riding and taking public transportation is competition because they are alternative transportation options.

Competition validates the market. It signals to investors that there is a problem that needs to be solved. As an entrepreneur, it's better to have some competition, rather than no competition at all, as competition signals that customers already spend time and/or money to solve the problem. Position yourself compared to the competition to demonstrate to customers, partners, and investors your differentiating factors. If there is no competition in your particular market, examine whether or not the market opportunity is as appealing as you may have originally thought.

38. So you're going to bet your future on someone else's opinion?

When you size your market, are you looking at analyst reports that estimate market size or other factors about your business? The "top down" market sizing approach may seem easy, but easy doesn't mean right or thoughtful. Insights gained from analyst reports are insights borrowed from someone else's mind. Sure, these reports can be useful and you should definitely read them, but don't build your business based on assumptions from someone else's opinion. Find out for yourself. Do customer discovery. Figure out the market need, what people are willing to pay, and so forth. Learn about your customers from the bottoms up so that you really understand your market, its metrics, and how best to execute.

Lesson for entrepreneurs:

Investors aren't fools (always) and can tell if you only read a market research report to build your assumptions. Do yourself a favor and take the time to do your own market research. Don't depend on the research done by consultants and others to inform your business building decisions.

39. Great feedback doesn't come from a vacuum.

In other words, get out of your office and talk to people, just as #36 suggests! Sitting in a room with your teammates sharing feedback about one of your products is akin to getting feedback from a vacuum. You're limiting yourself to a biased set of perspectives. Constructive feedback, which may be harsher, is typically the most helpful feedback in making positive changes to your product.

Lesson for entrepreneurs:

Go out and talk to people! Talk to current users of your product, potential future users, users of competing products, or others who may have another perspective.

40. Once you get them on the platform and using it, then you have to tell them why they should be using it, and you can sell them more stuff.

This statement illustrates the importance of a customer and building customer satisfaction and loyalty. Once you have customers using your platform and they recognize the value they derive from using it, doors open up. Happy customers become your best evangelists for acquiring new customers. Also, with those customers locked in using your product you know have the opportunity to sell them more products that will bring additional value.

Especially for specific market segments this can work wonderfully. For instance, consider a company that sells software to fitness studios. Its first product is the Trojan horse, a simple solution to a problem the studios face. Selling a product to those studios is no easy task, but once the studios try it out and recognize the benefits, they are hooked. Over time, the company builds a large customer base of hundreds and then thousands of fitness studios. The company has built a channel that can be used to sell more products to its existing customer base.

The other benefit of focusing on a market segment, building that base, and then "shoving more product down their throat" is that you learn a lot about that particular customer segments. For instance, using the previous example, in the process of selling the initial product to those fitness studios, the company learns a lot about those studios – the problems they face, their willingness to pay, their concerns, their buying process, and so forth. Considering "knowing your customer better than they know themselves" is another common piece of investor advice, it's not a bad thing to learn!

Lesson for entrepreneurs:

One approach to building your business is to create a product for a specific set of customers, get that segment of customers on board, and then find out what other products/services you can sell them. This strategy differs from selling the same product to different customer segments. Choose one, focus, and execute.

41. You cannot let your customer define your business model.

"Customer discovery" is valuable, but don't let your customer define your business model. The purpose of customer discovery is to learn more about the customers than they know about themselves. The danger in customer discovery is taking everything said by customers so literally that the customer ends up defining a business model.

Lesson for entrepreneurs:

Define your own business model. Use customer discovery to inform that business model, not decide it.

42. We can all sell stuff to our friends. Go out and sell to someone

you don't know.

I can't even count on my hands the number of times entrepreneurs' market validation consisted of sample sizes consisting of family members and friends. That doesn't count! Your family and friends are biased. They know you, they are supportive of you, and they want to see you succeed. They are a great sample to start with, but go find some unbiased people to really validate your market.

Lesson for entrepreneurs:

Test your idea with people you don't know and people who don't know you. Don't set up your experiment to achieve the results you want. The point of even testing a market is to make sure your idea has legs. The best way to do that is to test it against a **real** market.

> According to Steve Blank, the author of *The Four Steps to the Epiphany*, the Customer Development process "is the way startups quickly iterate and test each element of their business model, reducing customer and market risk. The first step of Customer Development is called Customer Discovery. In Discovery startups take all their hypotheses about the business model: product, market, customers, channel, etc. outside the building and test them in front of customers." Source: http://steveblank.com/2010/02/11/it-must-be-a-marketing-problem/

43. If you don't know what the customer is looking for how can you build them something?

Similarly, if you don't have a destination how are you going to get there? You're aimlessly wandering. Building to build will have you aimlessly wandering and spending more time and money to a probable dead end. Learn about your customer first and continue learning throughout the building process. The time spent learning about customers' needs will save you time and resources and improve your chances of creating a product that customers will actually want.

Lesson for entrepreneurs:

Know your customers better than they know themselves (Revisit #33 for more about knowing your customers).

44. If you're going to burn a market, burn one that no one gives a shit about.

At my former fund, we invested in a pre-product company that launched its beta product in a specific geographical market. At this early stage, the company was still figuring out its business model and it switched its business model several times, in the same geographical market. Its customers were faced with dealing with changes in pricing, pricing model, product features, among other characteristics. The company risked pissing off its customers with the changes, to the point at which the market would burn, or otherwise tire from all the changes and no longer be an attractive market for the company. It didn't matter though, because the lessons learned from running multiple experiments better positioned the company to launch in new markets with a much more refined service. Fortunately, the beta market didn't burn and the company was able to keep operating in the original test market while taking its model to other markets.

Lesson for entrepreneurs:

Choose a market in which to test your product/service. Choose it carefully. Choose a market that you can afford to burn, or toss out. Big cities like New York City or Los Angeles don't always make the best of test markets, especially if a large percent of your customer base is there. If you do test in a big market, roll out to a sample in that market, so there's still fresh customers to acquire after you refine your product/service. Execute in your chosen market(s). Run experiments on product, business model, and so forth. Take all you learn to launch in new markets, regardless of whether or not the initial market withstands the fires.

45. The roadside is littered with companies that tried to sell to the small and medium business (SMB) market.

There are many companies that fell by the roadside before achieving any market traction and distribution to the SMB market. SMBs are fragmented and difficult to reach. Distribution is key to selling to SMBs. Reaching them in a scalable way is key to building an economical model and a sustainable business.

Lesson for entrepreneurs:

If your customers are SMBs find some leverage in the model so you can get wider distribution and lower cost of customer acquisition. For example, if your customers are restaurants (*investor cringe*), can you partner with the National Restaurant Association or other entities to access many restaurants with one partnership? Find out who your customers already buy from or work with in some capacity, and then partner with them.

46. You don't need a beta product to demonstrate customer demand. And a survey isn't going to cut it.

One of the most regular questions I was asked while I was working at a venture capital firm was, "do you know any developers?" or something of the like. Everyone seemed to be looking for engineers. My response was similar to all – "Haven't you heard? They grow on trees!" In all reality, I would tell them to get in line because great engineering talent is high in demand. It continued to surprise me as to how many people would be looking to hire engineers before even testing the product/market fit.

Then there's the heightened interest in learning to code. Because if you learn to code you'll be able to build your own company, sell it to another company for millions of dollars and then retire in your thirties. Right. A few thoughts on that: 1) You do not need to know how to code in order to test your idea, and 2) Even if you do teach yourself to write code, or take a class/workshop, it will take lots of practice, work (and time) before you are really great enough to build a product/service for a multi-million dollar company you build on your own accord.

Before you look to hire engineers or teach yourself to code, test out your product/market with Wizard of Oz experiments aka ghetto testing aka testing hypotheses without writing any code (and oftentimes without even using online tools). These experiments are meant to test product/market without actually building your product. That's right, testing a product, without writing a single line of code. Sound impossible? It's not!

For instance, there once was a company that wanted to build a mobile app to enable small businesses to provide incentives for customers and allow customers to receive special deals and use a QR Code to redeem the incentives at the small businesses. Rather than actually build the app and see how (or if) people used it, the founders could have used Wizard of Oz experiments to test it out. They could have stood outside a small business handing out physical incentives to learn about consumer behavior around incentives, redemptions, types of deals most interesting to consumers, and other valuable insights previously unknown.

Lesson for entrepreneurs:

Before you look to hire engineers or teach yourself to code, follow the yellow brick road and test out your product/market with Wizard of Oz experiments. You'll save time, money, stress, and ultimately improve your product and story to investors if you choose to fundraise.

4 THE MODEL

The Model section dives into advice about business models and especially figuring out the viability of your model before scaling. Business models are not a thing of the past and are critical to building a scalable, sustainable business.

MARY LEMMER

47. All the factors of value proposition drive business model.

In an era where business models aren't always obvious, this piece of advice especially has value. The way in which your company makes money (or plans to make money) is important, especially to investors.

Struggling to figure out a business model? Experiment with business models driven by the value your product or service creates. Here's a quick way to determine some models to test:

1. Identify the core problem you're solving.
2. Charge for solving that problem.

Ta-dah! Now you have a business model!

For example, maybe babysitters struggle to manage their babysitting schedules, so an entrepreneur creates an online service to help babysitters organize their schedules. The problem being solved is babysitter scheduling. The business model experiment will discover – will babysitters pay for the online scheduling service? That's the business model: selling an online service to babysitters. Of course, pricing and the model in which you charge (e.g. freemium model, monthly subscription, transaction-based) must be determined as well, but experiments can also be used to test those pricing models.

Lesson for entrepreneurs:

Business models are not a thing of the past. If you are creating value, charge for it. Identify the problem you are solving and experiment with models to charge customers.

48. Track your experiments. Track results.

Experiments aren't useful if you aren't measuring results. Tracking results in your head is not a great place to keep them.

Some investors refer to the "clunk test" when doing diligence on investment opportunities. What's the "clunk test," you ask? If an entrepreneur has well documented experiments and results (along with other customer learning) in a binder, the binder, when dropped on the investor's desk will make a "clunk" noise. If the entrepreneur has put in enough work in understanding customers and running relevant experiments, that binder of data should be large enough to produce a "clunk."

If your binder is empty and you haven't been recording your experiments and customer learning, it's time to start! Not sure what or how to track your experiments and results? Here is a simple format to get you started:

Date: Date(s) of experiment
Experiment: Brief description about the experiment you're running
Hypothesis: Brief explanation about your anticipated results
Result: Actual results
Next step: Based on the results of the experiment, your plan going forward (e.g. run another experiment, adjust marketing message)

You may run dozens or hundreds or thousands of experiments. Excel tables are very useful in tracking experiments (and sharing them with others) in an organized fashion. Then you can categorize them by type of experiment, such as "marketing," "product," "business model," etc. Excel also allows you to easily filter to find experiment results and action items to share with relevant people, including investors. Refer to Figure 1 for an example of tracking experiments in Excel.

Figure 1. Experiment Tracking in Excel

Date	Experiment	Hypothesis	Result	Next Step
Date(s) of Experiment	Brief description about the experiment you're running	Brief explanation about what you think the results will be	Actual results	Based on the results of the experiment, your plan going forward

Other aspects you may want to track (depending on your particular situation):

- Person responsible for running the experiment
- Person responsible for analyzing the results of the experiment (to reduce biases great experiments have separate people running and measuring results of experiments)
- Category of experiment, because as you start running more and

more experiments it will be helpful to sort through experiments by type (e.g. Marketing Acquisition, Sales, Product Feature, Business Model, etc.)

Lesson for entrepreneurs:

Pass the "clunk test." Be organized and deliberate about tracking your experiments and results. Define a clear way to track results and also create a process to compile data into something that you can share with someone else (e.g. an investor doing diligence on your company or a new team member who needs to catch up to speed with previous efforts). With organized tracking you'll be well on your way to passing the "clunk test."

49. Know your model – if you put $X in, you will get how much out?

In the venture capital world, investors often refer to the X&Y formula: "x in equals y out." It is very important for entrepreneurs to know these numbers to understand their business model. It gives investors confidence that you understand your business and have thought about where money needs to be spent in order to generate value. It also helps entrepreneurs understand the potential scalability (or lack thereof) of their business.

For instance, a company selling an online service on a monthly subscription basis will want to measure its cost of customer acquisition and lifetime value of customers (among other metrics). Customer acquisition measures the "x" of the X&Y formula. The cost of customer acquisition includes every cost attributable to getting the prospect to become a customer, including expenses like advertising and travel to meet with prospects. There may be multiple costs of customer acquisition, depending on the channel used to acquire the customer (if you're running customer acquisition experiments and tracking them, you'll have a good sense for these numbers). Cost of customer acquisition through ads on Google may be more expensive than the cost of customer acquisition through a channel partner. Then, measure the value of the customers coming from each channel. How much are those customers paying you for your product or service on an ongoing basis? Track all of the acquisition costs and compare them to the value generated from those customers. When all is said and done, great entrepreneurs have enough information about their X&Y formula to be able to put together something like…

Channel	Cost of Customer Acquisition (X)	Value Generated (Y)
Google Ads	$4.00	$1.00/month $12/year
Partnership	$1.00	$1.00/month $12/year
Mailing Lists	$15.00	$1.00/month $12/year

Bonus points if you also include a column for "Number of Customers Generated" though you should be tracking this metric (as well as conversion rates) in your experiment log.

Looking at this example we can see that the most profitable way to acquire customers is through the partnership. On the flip side, purchasing mailing lists is not as profitable of a way to acquire customers. It takes longer for those customers to generate value. With this information you can tell investors that with the $100,000 you plan spend to acquire customers through partnerships you expect to generate $1.2 million in value over a year. Not only is this kind of information important to share with investors to give them confidence that your business model makes sense, but it also helps you identify where to invest money to scale your business. Imagine if you hadn't been tracking this information and you continued to spend money on acquiring customers through mailing lists. Yikes! You'd be bleeding a lot of money!

Lesson for entrepreneurs:

Measure the factors that make up your X&Y formula – for your investors and more importantly, for your company.

50. SaaS is not a buzzword. It's a way of doing business.

Software as a service, or SaaS as it's commonly referred to in the business, is a business model. It means what it says and implies that customers are paying for your company's software service. If you search for "SaaS definition" online, there will be plenty to read and learn more about what it is and how it works. One of my favorite definitions is from TechTarget:

Software as a Service (SaaS) is a software distribution model in which applications are hosted by a vendor or service provider and made available to customers over a network, typically the Internet.[1]

Couple that distribution model with a revenue model (i.e. charging customers for use of the software) and there you have it, a business model.

Lesson for entrepreneurs:

SaaS isn't a fad. It's a model for distribution and revenue generation. Use it.

51. Show me a business, not a product.

Not all products are businesses. All businesses sell products.

A *product*, by definition, is "something produced by human or mechanical effort or by a natural process."[2]

A *business*, by definition, is "an organization or economic system where goods and services are exchanged for one another or for money."[3]

> Ford is a business.
> Google is a business.
> A blender is a product.

A good rule of thumb to follow – you don't have a business until you have payroll. Until then, you're either working on a hobby and/or building a product. Products can lead to businesses. For instance, if you built a sophisticated blender and are selling these fancy blenders (products) you may grow into offering other kitchen devices and become a kitchen device company.

---

[1] http://searchcloudcomputing.techtarget.com/definition/Software-as-a-Service
[2] Source: www.Dictionary.com
[3] Source: www.BusinessDictionary.com

Keep in mind, if you're raising capital, it doesn't matter whether you consider your business a business and not a product, it matters what the folks with the money think. Demonstrate you have a business, so that the investors also believe you have a business.

Lesson for entrepreneurs:

Are you a product or a business? Investors back businesses, so if you're still a product figure out if there's a business there. Tell investors about the business you are building, not the product you are creating.

52. Facebook "likes" don't convert to revenue.

All the Facebook "likes" you have on your company's page are meaningless to your bottom line unless you have some ideas as to how to monetize those likes or otherwise measure the impact from the size of your audience.

For example, I know a guy who started a Facebook page around a popular drinking game and quickly racked up over one million "likes." How much money did he make from that spike? Nothing. Eventually he got some offers from companies to buy the page, but not for any significant amount of money (especially when you look at the amount as a "dollar per like" amount). Until he got creative with how to make money from his page, it wasn't pulling in any revenue. And even still, it's not a standalone business that investors were interested in backing.

The bottom line is, without a business model, even all the likes in the world won't get you much.

Lesson for entrepreneurs:

Share other more valuable metrics with investors. Or, if you have "eyeball metrics" like Facebook likes, support those numbers with some ideas to convert those eyeballs into dollars. The ideas could be unproven, as long as you demonstrate knowledge of a plan to test, measure, and iterate based on what you learn.

53. If you pivot more than once you're spinning in a circle.

If you have read *The Lean Startup* by Eric Ries, or anything about building "lean" then you probably have learned the term "pivot." Pivot is iteration based on learning what works and what doesn't work with your business. It's adjusting your business model or strategies to reflect new information you learn about your customers and market. It's great to get customer feedback early and adjust accordingly. Sometimes your entire business model or product will change. That's fine. Some great companies resulted from pivots. For instance, Twitter started as a podcasting business. Pandora was initially a B2B music recommendation service. YouTube was once a video dating website. Rather than pivot for pivoting sake, put some thought into your pivots. Keep them well informed and thoughtful.

For instance, say you start a business that offers an internet-based service that helps personal trainers find new clients. You test out your beta product and business model and quickly learn that personal trainers are unwilling to pay for a subscription service to help them find clients. You do learn that people who need personal trainers are more willing to pay for such a service to help them find quality personal trainers, so you shift your model to offer a website that helps people find quality personal trainers. And though your user research demonstrates that people will use this service to find personal trainers, not many seem willing to pay on a monthly basis. You test out several other business models (transaction based, freemium, free, and so forth), but ultimately none of them builds any significant traction. Do you keep pivoting the model? Or is the personal trainer market not interesting enough to pursue?

Lesson for entrepreneurs:

Remember, the more you pivot the more you are spinning in a circle. Be thoughtful about your pivots and be honest about when it's time to stop pivoting yourself to death.

5 THE PRODUCT

The Product section covers advice about testing, launching, and scaling products and/or services. Creating a product/service that people want is critical to building a standalone business.

MARY LEMMER

54. Create a sticky widget.

What's a sticky widget you may ask? Good question! I asked the same question when I first heard the term. A sticky widget is a product (or service) with addictive properties. "Sticky" meaning that it sticks…people use it and they use it a lot and are reluctant to change to use another product/service. And "widget" is the term we learn in economics class…something built, commonly used to refer to a product, but can also refer to a service.

Lesson for entrepreneurs:

Figure out what it is about your product or service that will be addicting for customers, making it difficult for customers to substitute your product or service with another. Make it stickier than cotton candy!

55. That time at the keyboard becomes so much more productive when it's backed by user-driven design. Now you know why you're coding.

When you're solving a problem for customers it's better to know about the customer before putting pen to paper (or fingers to keyboard in this case) to create a solution. Learning about the customer (again, back to #33, "know your customer better than they know themselves") can inform the user experience and features included in an early product.

Consider the flipside – you rush to build a first product to reach your customers, learn that the product is all wrong, the experience doesn't align with your customers' needs, and the features you included aren't important to them. Scrap that iteration and start from scratch.

Eventually, it is important to put a product out there, see how customers use it, get feedback, and iterate. But take some time before launching that first product to learn about customers to inform your early product development. The early customer discovery will spare you some time, resources, and make that first iteration more like a couple of tweaks instead of an entire reset.

Lesson for entrepreneurs:

Before writing any code, spend some time learning about your customers. Let the early learning inform your initial product development and continue to iterate as you get feedback on your products.

56. If it has a plug it's not getting funded.

This conclusion was reached by a wise, kite-surfing investor in March 2011, just before the annual South by Southwest (SXSW) took place. When considering SXSW and the Consumer Electronics Show (CES) another investor chimed in "CES is so 2001. SXSW is 2011." The CES used to be **the** place to be for anyone who's anyone in the technology space. Held annually in Las Vegas, tech entrepreneurs, innovators, investors were all certain to attend. Flash-forward about a decade later and SXSW is the new "it" place to be. Held each spring in Austin, Texas, SXSW combines music, technology, and movies for a lively 10 days of debauchery and "work." Many entrepreneurs will first launch new companies or products/services at SXSW since the festival is full of early adopters for new technology.

This shift in popular events mirrors the shift in investment focus and allocation.

Lesson for entrepreneurs:

If your product plugs into a wall be prepared to spend a decent amount of time explaining to investors about your customers and specifically around their willingness to pay for your product. Understand your product, market, your model, just like you would for any other type of business, but be prepared for some skepticism and interrogation.

57. There are no new ideas. It's all in the execution.

Ideas are worthless. Execution is everything. Investors back execution. Ideas are great, but worthless until acted upon.

Everything has been tried in some capacity. Ideas are built on, but none are truly new or novel. For instance, the self-driving car: the car is mobility. Mobility isn't a new idea. Driving a car is mobility. Riding passenger seat in a self-driving car is mobility. Nothing new, just evolved as technology advances and entrepreneurs pursue moving the idea forward.

Lesson for entrepreneurs:

Don't be scared to share your idea with people in fear that someone will steal it. If you are afraid of someone stealing your idea, it sends a signal that you are not a good executor.

Investors know that there are no new ideas, so don't pretend your idea has never been attempted before or doesn't already exist in some form or another. In doing so you will just demonstrate your naiveté and perhaps overconfidence. In some cases, it can also lessen the investors' trust in you.

58. It's not always the best product that wins. It's the best distribution.

Some of the coolest products never make it to the mainstream market, mostly because of poor distribution. Poor distribution can be a result of poor marketing, strategy, and/or business development. Marketing and distribution can make all the difference. It will make all the difference. Because even the best products aren't guaranteed to just be discovered without some active marketing and efficient distribution.

Some distribution is more effective than others. When you are trying to reach a large, distributed customer base, it is rarely effective to go knocking on individual doors to tell them about your product/service. Rather, find what investors refer to as "leverage in the model," partners who already have your target customers in their audience. For instance, if your company's customers are small to medium businesses (SMBs), rather than sending feet on the street to go to each SMB and tell them about your product/service, figure out who already reaches a lot of SMBs and then figure out a way to partner with them. Other businesses, trade associations, conferences, suppliers, and other entities are a good place to start when figuring out potential partners. Figure out how you can help the partner as well, otherwise it will be a tough road to convince them to connect your company with the valuable customer/member base they've already generated.

For instance, Facebook was not the first online social network. Friendster and MySpace preceded Facebook, yet Facebook has outgrown its competitors. It is argued that Facebook's distribution, through select college campuses, was instrumental in its ability to become **the** social network of choice.

Lesson for entrepreneurs:

Don't underestimate the importance of distribution. Be ready to share with investors how you will reach customers in an economically viable fashion.

59. Create an illusion of bigness.

Maybe you're a small company. That doesn't mean outsiders need to perceive you as small. There are ways to create an illusion of bigness, or make yourself seem like a larger organization than you actually are. How? Here are some ideas to start:

- **Generate significant and positive press.** Just one feature in an article in the Wall Street Journal, New York Times, or other popular publication for your industry, makes you seem as if you're a "real" company. Even if you're still two people with an idea to test and minimum viable product to experiment with, you'll create the illusion of bigness by getting featured in some good press.
- **Design a great user interface and user experience that is slick.** If your website looks professional people will consider you professional. You don't have the best website out there, but make it look good and be functional, so that your audience doesn't question the trustworthiness of your site, brand, and company.

Why is this useful? Perception is reality, so if you appear to know what you're doing, you'll gain the trust of more customers, investors, and potential hires. Landing large customers requires their trust on your ability to deliver, and often times that trust is correlated with the perception of your size.

Lesson for entrepreneurs:

Perception is reality. Behind the scenes may need improvement, but create the illusion of bigness by generating some good press and creating a user experience that is slick and major-bug free and you'll gain trust with customers, investors, and others.

60. Sell scarcity.

The psychology behind this is simple. When we know there is a short supply of something, it becomes more appealing. Think about it with shopping: If there are only 10 widgets left, positioning those widgets as "last 10 available" will increase the urgency for customers to buy them before the widgets are gone. A customer thinks "I better get there and buy a widget before they run out." Black Friday is a great example of this psychological heuristic in action. There are only so many deals available for a limited amount of time, influencing customers to camp outside retailers in order to ensure they get the deals.

Lesson for entrepreneurs:

Try selling scarcity and see how it impacts your sales and customer engagement. Test, measure, evaluate. It may be a tactic worth keeping.

61. Owning inventory is so 1990s.

If your company holds inventory and/or makes products that plug into a wall (discussed in #56), be prepared for investors to either a) run, b) run fast, or c) ask a **ton** of questions during diligence (asking questions and running are not mutually exclusive, by the way). Don't get me wrong, some investors focus on hardware or are logistics and physical product gurus, but regardless, if you are holding inventory, know your stuff – How are you going to do it? Learn about the best ways to manage inventory, create a plan to manage it and make it efficient enough to not jeopardize margins significantly and/or scare investors until they run for the hills.

Lesson for entrepreneurs:

Live in the 21st century. And if you are going to hold inventory, spend time running the economics of owning and managing inventory and build your team with competent people to understand the best ways to manage inventory.

6 THE FUNDRAISE

The Fundraise section includes advice about how best to tell your story to investors as well as some tips around structuring a deal with investors. It's not as scary as it seems.

MARY LEMMER

62. The best pitches are not pitches. They are conversations.

If an investor pulls you out of your pitch, you're in good shape. It's usually not a good sign if you get through your entire pitch without the investor saying anything. In fact, she/he may even be sleeping (a reason to always take a meeting in person versus via phone, if you have the choice). When an investor starts to ask questions, share ideas, and generally engage in conversation about your business, that demonstrates her/his interest in your company.

If a pitch starts and ends without commentary or questions from the investor, the pitch is a pitch. And pitches don't get funded. Conversations and well-told stories by talented storytellers get funded.

What does that mean for you? First, throw out the word "pitch." Stop thinking of your meetings with investors as "pitches" and start thinking of them as conversations and the opportunity to share your story with people who may be able to help you. Then, craft your story to engage the audience in conversation. You'll be glad you did.

Here's a story to illustrate the impact of storytelling. When I was mentoring students in a student start-up accelerator, one of the students asked if she could share her pitch and get my feedback. I listened to her pitch for a company selling warming gloves. Her pitch was very technical, dry, and informative (filled with market stats). It was fine, but it wasn't compelling. It wasn't grabbing. There was no story. If my attention span were just half of the average investor, I would not have made it through listening to her entire pitch fully engaged. Her product, warming gloves, was conducive to telling a great, compelling story. I shared my feedback and challenged her to ditch the pitch and tell a story. After recharging, she came back to me and shared her story. She opened her story with a photo of a man sitting in freezing weather, after experiencing the earthquake and tsunami in Japan in 2011. She told the story of this man – alone, cold, lost from his family, and his hands about to fall off from the frost bite. As the audience, I am emotionally drawn to her story. I am interested in learning more. She told the story to make the problem stand out as compelling, so that her solution, warming gloves, seem that much more important. The rest of her story flowed well and she included the relevant data and statistics to provide evidence of the market opportunity, but ultimately, it was her attention grabbing storytelling that started the conversation about how the investor and entrepreneur can work together to make this happen.

Another aspiring entrepreneur shared his pitch for a gluten-free cookie company, opening with a statistic about the increasing number of allergies. Little did he know that I have a gluten-intolerance and could relate to everything he was explaining. Had he known, he could have started a conversation with me long before the conversation started (when he finally breathed and I could mention my situation). I am very emotionally connected to the problem he was solving. All it took was him asking me a few questions or trying to get to know me better before jumping into his pitch.

As much as you can, get to know investors before sharing your story with them. A meeting with an investor doesn't need to immediately start with you diving into the presentation you prepared. It also doesn't need to start with talking about the weather. Maybe ask about her/his weekend, comment on a recent newsworthy event, and even better to ask questions related to the problem your company solves, to find out if the investor has ever experienced such problems or can relate in any way (of course, likelihood of relating will depend on the type of problem you're solving). Engage investors early to improve your likelihood of keeping them engaged longer.

Lesson for entrepreneurs:

Ditch the pitch. Tell a story. Spend some time getting to know who you are sharing your story with because you never know when you'll hit on some common ground that will influence how you tell your story. Remember, your story doesn't need to sound the same to every person you tell because, ultimately, great stories are great conversations, and conversations aren't always the same.

63. You have to build a crescendo into fundraising. Build your story.

Great entrepreneurs are great storytellers. As an entrepreneur you are always telling your story – to investors, to customers, to potential hires, to random people on planes and elevators, and so forth. Fundraising is storytelling, with an ask, to investors. Create a compelling story. Without a great story you are less likely to raise money. Investors invest in great stories, as explained in #62.

Lesson for entrepreneurs:

Test, measure, evaluate, and share the results from your experiments.

Run enough experiments to gather metrics to support your story and build a investor-backable story. Cost of customer acquisition declining. Average sales price increasing. Engagement building. Partnerships closing (actually closing). Those are messages in stories that peak investors' interests.

64. For everything you say in an elevator pitch, there should be some reason you're putting it there.

Sometimes less is more. It's an elevator pitch, so by definition it's short and to the point (Unless your elevator gets stuck – but don't make that assumption). Include only what you need to pique interest. Most of the best elevator pitches are short – short stories that describe your business and the value you provide to customers. Elevator pitches are meant to last elevator rides up short distances, not up the Sears tower. The more elaborate your pitch becomes, the less likely your audience will remember all what you told them. Stick to the key points your audience cares about learning. For investors, this means team, product, market, and traction. For a customer, hit your value propositions.

In theory, investors typically hold weekly partners meetings during which the team shares about the interesting companies they connected with during the week. If your story isn't clear and memorable the partner (or more likely, associate) you spoke with may not share the story in a positive way that really gets your message across in a way that you prefer. Think of the game of "telephone" – you start with a message, share it with someone else, who then shares it with another person, and so forth. By the time the message reaches the end it's rarely the same message. The clearer, simpler your message is to the partner or associate you speak with, and the more engaged and interested they are in your story, the more likely they will share your story in a similar fashion.

Remember, the goal of an elevator pitch is for your audience to understand what you are talking about and to inspire interest to get that next meeting. Keep key messages in your back pocket for short, to the point, effective encounters with individuals in elevators!

Think of it in terms of dating, because all good entrepreneurial advice comes with its own dating analogy: On the first date you're not trying for a proposal. You're looking to get a second date.

Lesson for entrepreneurs:

As you craft your elevator pitch (or any pitch for that matter), storyboard your presentation. Stick one message per slide. Keep it simple. Simple is memorable and you want to be memorable!

Be deliberate. Get that second date.

65. If you screw up your pitch, don't say anything at the end. Most likely your audience won't notice.

Just like live plays or concerts, the audience doesn't notice the tiny details that the performers notice. Button undone? Chord played wrong? You may notice and so may the others on your team, but the likelihood of the audience noticing is much less. The audience is there to watch you and is less knowledgeable about the details that you have been preparing to take to the stage.

Of course, there may always be a few folks in the audience who pick out the little things that go wrong. Those people are in the minority though.

Lesson for entrepreneurs:

Roll with the punches. If you mess up a word, or stutter, or otherwise mix up your pitch, let it go and just keep going! Most of the time your audience won't notice that you slipped and you can always course correct later. Be nimble and flexible to be ready for anything that comes your way.

66. If I don't get it, it's your fault, not mine.

If an investor doesn't understand what you're explaining, it is your fault, not the investor's fault, and that is how the investor will perceive it. Even if you're explaining quantum physics or some other very complex topic, it's your job to explain whatever the topic in a clear and compelling fashion. If your audience doesn't understand, they aren't going to move forward. Investors won't invest. Customers won't buy. Take time to consider your audience and craft your story accordingly.

Lesson for entrepreneurs:

Tell your story well! Know your audience and craft your story in a way that is understandable and appealing to that audience.

67. A deck has to stand alone without a story because it will circulate throughout the firm.

Put yourself in an investor's shoes. They see a lot of pitches, learn about a lot of companies, and have very short attention spans. Keep in mind the audience when you send a deck to an investor. Make it easy for investors to understand your story just from the deck. Keep it simple, short, and straight to the point. As far as the Steve Jobs' style presentation…save that for an in-person pitch when you can add commentary to the visual story.

Lesson for entrepreneurs:

Keep your deck short, simple, and easy to understand quickly. The easier it is for investors to understand your story from your deck (without you telling the story) the more likely you are to be invited to share your story with investors in person.

68. If I go like this it means go faster.

When sharing your story with investors (because great entrepreneurs don't pitch, they tell stories, as discussed in #62) pay attention to body language and non-verbal cues, in addition to verbal cues. A couple behaviors to look out for when chatting with investors:

Is the investor...

- Rolling her/his eyes?
- Spinning a pen/pencil/stylus?
- Using her/his phone?
- Typing on her/his computer without regularly looking up at you?

If you answer "yes" to any or all of those behaviors then guess what?! The investor is not paying attention to you. You will not raise money from them. You will not pass Go. You will not collect $200.

If you notice these behaviors, don't lose hope completely. Your sudden shift from realizing what's going on will not make the situation any better. Rather, consider doing something to recapture the investor's attention. Some ideas:

- Jump into a product demo (if you have one) or give an illustrative example.
- Stop and ask if there are any questions.
- Ask the investor a question.
- Stop talking. The silence will at least catch attention.
- Start singing, instead of speaking, what you're saying.

Ok, so the last tip is a bit extreme, but guaranteed to catch attention!

Lesson for entrepreneurs:

Be creative. Be aware. Act accordingly.

69. "I think" isn't good enough. You should "know."

When an investor asks about market size or demand, responding "I think…" demonstrates a lack of confidence and understanding of your market. This piece of wisdom also relates to #33, "Know your customer better than they know themself." If you don't know, admit it, but have an idea for how you will learn. When you find yourself **thinking**, figure out what you need to do to **know**.

Lesson for entrepreneurs:

Again, it all goes back to knowing your customers and learning about your market. Also, avoid excessive use of "I think" when telling your story to investors. At the same time, don't pretend to know things that you don't know. No one has all the answers. Use humility to recognize what you don't know and spend time figuring out what you need to do to "know" what you, at the time, "think."

Be real with investors and do as much of your homework ahead of time, so you can "know" rather than "think." If you don't know something, recognize it, and understand the steps you will take to learn it, as investors may be interested in understanding those steps too.

70. You can lie with statistics, but you can't deny the facts.

The only required reading one of the VC partners assigned me was the book, *How to Lie with Statistics* by Darrell Huff. Why? Well a lot of entrepreneurs include graphs and data in their presentations, and those graphs and data aren't always telling the real truth. It's easy to twist data to tell a story that you want to tell, as opposed to telling the real story that hides behind the data. Part of an investor's job during diligence is to cut through the crap, ask a lot of questions, and poke holes in assumptions.

Reading *How to Lie with Statistics* helped me understand the various ways statistics can be reshaped and better prepared me to ask the tough questions to entrepreneurs. It also has useful tips and tricks for using data to tell the story you want to tell, with some embellishment usually involved.

As an entrepreneur it is useful to understand how to twist data to tell a story you want to tell, especially when building your fundraising story. Not everyone is keen to asking the questions about the data, so understanding how to reshape statistics can help you make compelling arguments supporting the market opportunity you are pursuing. That being said, I don't condone lying with statistics, because even though you can lie with statistics, you cannot deny the facts. Be cautious about twisting statistics to tell a truth that doesn't exist, because even if you can convince others the story is true, if it's not, you're just fooling yourself.

Lesson for entrepreneurs:

Challenge the statistics you see about your market and be prepared for investors to challenge any and all statistics you share. Though you can use statistics to formulate the story you want to tell, best to be honest with yourself and the data. Otherwise, at the end of the day you're the only fool left standing.

71. What are the three most important things the company must do to prove you can tackle the market?

Be prepared to answer this question to investors. Even if they don't ask you, know the answer. It's important for you as an entrepreneur to understand what the three most critical items and it demonstrates your understanding of the market to investors.

Equally important – ensure your team knows the answer to this question as well. When you ask members of your team, do their answers align with yours? They should. If not, improve communication and align perceptions. The more in sync your team is about this topic the better off you'll be and the more likely you'll be able to pass diligence meetings with investors.

Lesson for entrepreneurs:

Know the answer to this question and make sure your team knows as well.

72. A business plan is a static document and there's no such thing as a static startup.

VCs don't read business plans.

Lesson for entrepreneurs:

Send a short deck with sharp messages that investors can look through in minutes, not hours. Avoid sending business plans or offering to send a business plan, unless an investor specifically asks for it.

That's not to say that business plans are not useful. They can be helpful for entrepreneurs to put together as it forces you to think through many aspects of your business. Though a business plan will not prepare you for the unexpected situations that inevitably will come up when building your business, the plan will force you to think through a lot about your business and can better prepare you for the road ahead.

73. Over half of fundraising is timing. (Finding a partner when they have bandwidth, timing for partner's fund, etc.)

You can practice your pitch day in and day out and still not raise capital. You may have a great team, fantastic product, in a large and underserved market, and still not raise capital.

"Wait, you're telling me that I can be sitting on a perfect opportunity and still not raise capital?!"

Yes, yes I am.

Why? Because timing is a huge factor in fundraising. Investor timing. Timing means:

- finding a partner when she/he has bandwidth;
- approaching a fund when they still have capital to invest and are looking for companies of your size/scope;
- raising capital during the best times of year for fundraising (i.e. not holidays)

Lesson for entrepreneurs:

Timing can have everything to do with your inability to raise capital. Optimize your timing as much as you can in your control and be aware of investor timing and fund/partner circumstances.

74. We don't sign NDAs because it is for the entrepreneurs' protection.

Investors don't sign nondisclosure agreements (NDAs) for several reasons. Mainly, it **protects investors and entrepreneurs.** Investors look at a lot of companies. It's their job. So at any one time an investor could be looking at several companies tackling a similar problem or offering a similar product. What happens if Company A gets funded and Company B does not? If the investor signed NDAs for both companies, Company B may claim the investor stole her/his idea and funded Company A.

It's not practical for entrepreneurs or investors to sign NDAs. Really, when was the last time a VC stole an entrepreneur's idea? Remember, ideas are worthless. It's all about execution. Great VCs don't spend time stealing entrepreneurs' ideas and running several ideas into the ground. That's not their business. More importantly, the venture industry is built solely on trust. If that happened it's likely that a VC wouldn't be a popular capital choice among savvy entrepreneurs.

The entire NDA process also **takes time.** Investors would need to have their attorney review the language. The attorney will probably propose changes (billable hours!) and it could be weeks before the NDA is even signed and the entrepreneur is "able" to tell the investor about her/his business.

Lesson for entrepreneurs:

Don't ask an investor to sign an NDA. It shows naiveté and inexperience on the entrepreneur's part.

75. We don't invest unless we can add value.

For an early stage venture capital investor it's logical to make investments in companies when more than money can help the company progress.

Investors want to do everything they can to add value to the company because the more valuable the company, the better our chances for a return on their investment. Keep in mind, not every investor's model is the same, so some investors may not care as much about adding value beyond capital.

Lesson for entrepreneurs:

Many investors will say they "add value." Test for yourself whether or not that is true. Talk to other portfolio company CEOs, get to know the partners, and really understand what they do for their companies. Figure out what you're looking for and make sure that aligns with the investors' expectations. Also, don't be afraid to ask your investors for help, especially if they claim they'll add value. Great investors are your partners and want to help. Recognize whether the investor intends to add value beyond capital and prepare accordingly.

76. We won't invest in a company that we wouldn't want to work in as entrepreneurs.

Venture capital is one of the rare jobs where you pick everyone you work with: your investors (referred to as "limited partners"), your partners, and your investments.

This line comes loudest from early stage investors and former operators. They like to get their hands dirty. They have experience in the trenches and may enjoy living vicariously through the entrepreneurs they help. By choosing to invest in companies they'd like to work in as entrepreneurs, they are choosing to be on your team and help you in those trenches when things are going well and not so well.

Lesson for entrepreneurs:

Build relationships. VCs want to work with people they know, trust, and want to spend time with during many hours of the day. Part of investors' diligence process is figuring out if they want to work with the entrepreneur(s). As an entrepreneur, it is important for you to do the same. You can pick your investors (even if you have few or one option, you always have the option to say no). Find investors you feel comfortable calling with good news or bad news.

Diligence (noun) "1. An investigation or audit of a potential investment. Due diligence serves to confirm all material facts in regards to a sale. 2. Generally, due diligence refers to the care a reasonable person should take before entering into an agreement or a transaction with another party" (Source: Investopedia).

Investors perform what is commonly referred to as "diligence" when deciding whether to make an investment or not. Diligence often involves investors meeting the team, hearing the company's story, evaluating the company's model, digging through company's financials/projects, learning about the market, making reference calls, performing background checks on the founders, visiting the company's office, among other activities. The diligence process can take barely any time at all or stretch on for months, years even. The length of time for diligence is heavily dependent on how well the investor knows the entrepreneur and understands the business already.

---

77. We don't believe in overcapitalizing companies. We believe in capitalizing them enough, and holding money in reserve.

There are some advantages to having enough money, but not so much that money is spent on unnecessary expenses. Less money forces more discipline in spending. Less money also forces focus on key goals and prioritization of milestones that need to be achieved. Plus, when entrepreneurs raise more money than they need to reach a key milestone, they can lose the opportunity to raise more money at a higher valuation (after making progress from raising some capital earlier).

Lesson for entrepreneurs:

Know how much money you absolutely need. Use that information to figure out the amount to raise now, the milestones you aspire to reach with that capital, and how much money you expect to raise in the future.

78. There is no science for valuing companies. There are tools.

One of my responsibilities at RPM Ventures was to work with our accountants and auditors to put together our annual valuation report at the end of the year. Business school classes teach formulaic valuation methodologies including discounting cash flows and evaluating comparable companies. However, these methodologies don't cleanly apply to valuing early stage companies. Let's consider the various valuation methodologies taught in business school:

- *Discounting cash flows.* What cash flows? 80 percent of our investments at RPM Ventures not only were pre-revenue companies, they were also pre-product companies! The only cash flows to track were negative cash flows. Even cash flow projections are just that – projections – and not an accurate representation of the future. Thus, the discounted cash flow (DCF) valuation methodology was not the most useful tool.

- *Evaluating comparable companies.* This valuation technique can be more useful than DCF, yet how can you accurately compare a small privately held company that is pre-revenue and pre-product to a large, publicly-held company with hundreds of millions if not billions of dollars in revenue? You can look at price to earnings multiples, apply those to any earnings, discount the results due to differences in liquidity, and come up with a number or range. Of course, that assumes you have revenues to multiply (because $0 times anything is still $0). Evaluating comparable company transactions can be quite helpful. For instance, if Google acquired a similar private company for $300 million and that company was generating $30 million revenue annually, that 10x revenue multiplier can be used to estimate the value of your company. The trouble with using comparable transactions is, again, if your company doesn't have revenue, you have nothing to multiply, and a lot of acquisition transaction data is not publicly available.

So if the traditional business school valuation methodologies don't necessarily apply, how do investors decide on what your company is worth? What determines the valuation that makes it to the term sheet? Valuation is an art. There is no single methodology or formula to figure it out. I have seen the following factors influence the determination of company value:

- *Horse, jockey, race* (or the team, product, and market). These are generally the elements investors look for when deciding on whether or not to make an investment. The faster your horse, more experienced your jockey, and bigger your race, the higher your valuation.

- *Traction and milestones achieved so far.* How well do you know your customers? Do you have pre-orders? Has there been demonstrated interest in paying for your product/service? What has the team accomplished since inception? These are some of the questions investors will ask to better understand the team's traction and what they have accomplished already.

- *Previous capital raised.* Not only is it important for investors to consider traction and achievements so far, but investors will also want to know how much it cost to reach those milestones. Knowing this gives investors a sense of the team's capital efficiency (or lack thereof).

- *Investors' ownership hurdles.* Some investors must achieve a certain level of ownership in order to make an investment. When this is the case, the cap table is built up to figure out what the post-money valuation needs to be in order for the investor to meet its requirement.

- *Relationship.* When investors know the entrepreneur(s) the valuation can be impacted accordingly.

Lesson for entrepreneurs:

Your company is not worth $100 million. This I promise you. Your company is probably worth a lot less than what you think it is worth. Understand that there are several factors investors consider when deciding on your company's valuation. You can use some valuation tools to try and put a number value on your company, but don't be shocked when investors' valuations are much different than yours. Remember, valuation is an art, not a science.

79. Investors care about post-money.

Why? Because post-money affects investors' ownership and ultimately, their payday.

Take this scenario: You raise $2 million in Series A capital, in a round with a $3 million pre-money valuation. That means your post money valuation is $5 million ($3 million + $2 million). For simplicity let's assume three investors are investing capital in the $2 million round. The lead investor (Investor A) puts in $1 million and the other two investors (B and C) both put in $500,000. The pre money capitalization table ("cap table") may look something like this:

	Number of Shares	Percent Ownership
Common Shares	5,000,000	100%

As part of the financing, the investors also want to create a 20% option pool. Along with the new investment, the cap table will look like:

	Number of Shares	Percent Ownership
Common Shares	5,000,000	40%
New Option Pool	2,500,000	20%
New Preferred Shares	5,000,000	40%
Total	*12,500,000*	*100%*

The percent ownership for the Series A investors is found by dividing the total investment ($2 million) by the post-money valuation ($5 million), so in this case 40% ($2 million / $5 million). At the end of the day, this post-money ownership will impact investors' potential earnings. The higher the post-money ownership, the better off the investor is when the company is sold or goes public. Since early stage investors face the risk of getting diluted in future investment rounds and when the company is sold, fully diluted ownership plays a significant role in determining the investors' returned capital.

Lesson for entrepreneurs:

Understand the jargon. Consider post-money. It's what matters.

Think about the return an investor needs to have to return capital to their investors and work back from there. By thinking like an investor you're likely to align goals, get a good valuation, and a great partner.

80. Right way to get a term sheet done: start by agreeing you want to do the deal. Wrong way: start by negotiating details.

Let me paint a hypothetical situation for you...

You recently decided you needed to raise capital to take your business to the next level. For the past six weeks you have been actively fundraising, regularly meeting with angel investors and venture capitalists. So far all you have received is some advice and bottled water souvenirs from your meetings. Finally, you find the investor you dream of working with and she/he is interested in investing in your business. It feels almost too good to be true. A match made in Heaven.

Now comes the "choose your own adventure" part of this hypothetical situation. After you and the investor have both expressed interest in working together and the investor sends you a term sheet do you...

a) Sign the term sheet
b) Set up a time to talk to the investor via phone or in person to discuss the deal
c) Respond to the investor with a list of your proposed changes

What did you choose? If you chose adventure c) you have two seconds to change your mind.

Let's walk through these options. First, option a). Signing the term sheet, as is, is perfectly acceptable, and highly encouraged if you like the investor and the terms. However, if the terms aren't aligned with your expectations you may want discuss your concerns with the investor. How best to do this? Call her/him up or set up a time to meet in person to discuss the term sheet.

Lesson for entrepreneurs:

Once you and an investor decide that you want to work together, the devil is in the details. But don't turn the details into the devil.

81.   Don't agree to anything until deal is closed.

It's like the old saying goes, "it's not over until the fat lady sings." Well a deal isn't closed until it's signed, so don't assume it's done when it's not. Entrepreneurs get themselves into binds, especially financial binds, if they jump the gun and assume deals will close that don't end up closing.

For instance, imagine your company produces and sells a food product through wholesale channels and you are deep in negotiations with the largest wholesaler for your particular product. The conversations are going well and the wholesaler has shared with you the quantity it will purchase in its first order, providing you with confidence that the deal will close. In order to fulfill such a large order your company will need to ramp up production, requiring several thousand dollars worth of equipment and upgrades. If you make the upgrades before the deal is signed you risk the deal not closing and you're left with either loads of debt you cannot service or less cash to operate and grow, or other financial constraints (depending on how you financed your company). But if you wait until the deal is signed you risk not being prepared to deliver the first order, as it will take weeks to prepare for that level or production. What do you do?

Wait until your chickens hatch before you count them. Or, if you need to count them before, proceed cautiously and be aware of the consequences of your over or underestimating.

Lesson for entrepreneurs:

When you're confident a deal will close, take a step back and consider the risks involved with making big decisions that are influenced by the deal. If at all possible, wait until the deal is signed to spend resources to prepare accordingly.

82.   Money is a resource for entrepreneurs, but time is more precious. The math: money will not solve all your problems. To think so is folly.

Time is money and there is only so much time in the day. Raising capital is not an ends, it's a means. Capital provides a resource to build your business, but money without time is worthless. Once money is raised, time is all you need. Time to hire more people. Time to run experiments. Time to meet with customers. Time to continue to build relationships with new investors. Time to spend with existing investors (updates, board meetings).

Raising money will not make everything you need to spend your time doing disappear. It will only add to the list of things you need to do.

Lesson for entrepreneurs:

Keep time sacred.

7 THE LIFE

The Life section includes advice about living the life as an entrepreneur and investor. Life as an entrepreneur is more than about work. Think of life as entrepreneur holistically, in that it touches many aspects of your life beyond just the time spent with your company.

83. If it were easy everybody would be doing it.

Movies like *The Social Network*, blog posts about companies selling for millions (and billions) of dollars, and stories of rich and famous young entrepreneurs with their comfortable lifestyles create a perception of what it's like to be an entrepreneur. That's exactly what they are – perceptions. Perceptions created by media's stories about the sexy parts of being an entrepreneur. Truth is, building companies is a grind. It's hard work and rarely luxury and glamour.

Being an entrepreneur isn't something you choose. It chooses you. It isn't a job. It's a lifestyle. It is stressful, time-consuming, and risky. Don't get me wrong, it can also be incredibly rewarding. But the reward comes with a price.

Starting companies is easy.
Building companies is hard.

Legally, starting a company is fairly straightforward. Incorporate, put up a website, figure out what you're selling.

Building a company involves putting together a team, selling more of your product/service, handling customer service, setting up payroll and other administrative necessities, possibly raising capital, firing people, putting out fires, continuing to develop your product/service. All within 24 hours each day.

I have met plenty of successful entrepreneurs who make huge sacrifices to pursue their venture. Financial sacrifices. Personal sacrifices. You won't find every entrepreneur sleeping on couches or eating ramen, but each entrepreneur carriers her/his own sacrifices when pursuing an entrepreneurial venture. It's not easy.

Lesson for entrepreneurs:

Don't expect building a company to be easy because it's not. Prepare yourself for the ride of your life and enjoy the process.

84. Once you take investor money you have a responsibility to them more than just their money.

I learned this lesson as it relates to VCs raising money from their

Limited Partners (LPs). VCs have more than a fiduciary responsibility to their investors. Not legally, but informally. For instance, if an LP asks for an introduction to someone the VC knows or asks for a reference letter for her/his son for a job, the VC will do it. It's the right thing to do and it strengthens the relationship.

Similarly, as a venture-backed entrepreneur, if your investor asks you to talk to her/his son about your alma matter, or asks if you know an accountant in your hometown, you respond. You do what you can to help. It's the right thing to do and part of the unwritten ethos of the industry.

Lesson for entrepreneurs:

Once you take investor money you have a responsibility to investors more than just to return their money. Consider the relationship and the informal agreements made when you raise capital, and prepare accordingly.

85. Sometimes luck is your best ally.

Even with all the talent in the world, sometimes a little luck is all it takes to reach success.

Look at a company like Google, for example. Many early Googlers went off to start their own companies, and they had the "Google badge of honor" and a success under their belt that makes investors drool. Did early Googlers know that Google would become as valuable as it did? At the time, probably not. There is no such thing as a sure thing. They could calculate the pros/cons/likelihood of success all day, but at some point, when deciding to join a company or start a company, you must have some faith in the idea, team, problem being solved by your particular product/services. At some point you jump in, not knowing what the outcome will be. That's when luck can come into play. You may get a bit lucky, having chosen the right pool to jump in. Or, maybe you learn that you jumped in the pool with the murky waters and the pool you didn't jump in was the pool full of gold.

Lesson for entrepreneurs:

Be opportunistic. And don't beat yourself up if things don't go as you planned.

86. Don't count your chickens before they hatch.

You have probably heard this saying before, applied to other contexts. It holds true for entrepreneurs as well.

- *Raising money?* The deal isn't closed until the documents are signed and the money isn't in the bank until it's in the bank.
- *Customer interest?* Someone is not a customer until the dotted lines are signed and the customer has paid.
- *Sold your company?* Similar to raising money, the deal isn't closed until the docs are signed and the money isn't in the bank until it's in the bank.

Successful entrepreneurs don't build companies off of hope and wishes. Real stuff needs to happen!

For instance, often times when a company is considering acquiring another company, the diligence process takes time. Even though it may seem like a sure thing that the company will complete the acquisition, with early stage companies (and in life), there is no such thing as a sure thing. Imagine you tell a bunch of people, including the press, that Facebook is going to acquire your company...and then they don't. Have fun explaining that one.

Lesson for entrepreneurs:

Wait until the dotted line is signed before firing off the press releases.

87. Don't sign leases for more than two years.

Especially with early stage companies, nothing is guaranteed. The company may shut down after six months. At anytime something can blow up and to be locked into a lease limits quick liquidation options. Obviously there are always options in case something comes up, but best to start with small commitments and make larger ones when there is more certainty.

Lesson for entrepreneurs:

Pay attention to the financial commitments you make early on. Though it may seem like you'll be operating for years down the road (that's the intention!) keep in mind that starting a company is a risky endeavor, filled with ups and downs. Be smart up front by avoiding long term financial commitments that will come back to haunt you in case all doesn't go as planned.

88. The worst way to negotiate is to make an assumption about how people are going to negotiate.

As soon as you put an idea into your head as to how someone is going to communicate with you, you set preconceived notions that may or may not be true. In doing this you can lose touch with the reality of the situation and take yourself out of the present. To be an effective negotiator you must stay in the present.

Lesson for entrepreneurs:

Don't make assumptions. Enter negotiations well informed about the negotiating partner and with an open mind to listen, learn, and react in the moment.

89. Expectations are a source of disappointment.

This advice is also true in life. Think about it. Think about a time you had big expectations. If those expectations are met, great! If not, disappointment results. Without expectations, disappointment is less likely to be a consequence.

For instance, for an entrepreneur, expecting an investor to invest can very likely lead to disappointment if the investor does not invest. Work hard to convince the investor to invest, but do not create expectations that will lead you to disappointment.

Lesson for entrepreneurs:

Have no expectations and results will always exceed them. Or, better yet, manage your expectations and be realistic.

90. So many entrepreneurs think board meetings are mystical, and they make a big deal of them. All the real work is done behind the scenes. Board meetings are actually really boring.

Board meetings are called board meetings for a reason. Aside from the occasional joke or interludes of fun, board meetings are fairly informational and may be considered boring by some standards. During the board meetings the company updates investors and board members on the status of the company and discussion ensues. It essentially is a review with glimpses of strategic discussion (the balance depends on the company and stage especially). The real work happens between the board meetings. The board meetings help to identify opportunities where board members can help, and then in between board meetings board members do the work (making introductions, working on specific projects, diving deeper into an area of the business and so forth).

Lesson for entrepreneurs:

If you're spending more time working on presentations for your board meetings than you are spending working on your business, reconsider how you are allocating your time. Similarly, if all of your requests and discussions of problems and opportunities are happening during the board meetings, you're in trouble. Consider building better relationships with your board members, so that you are communicating with them between board meetings and the board meetings involve less of those conversations that should be taking place outside of the boardroom. The more you save to discuss during the board meetings, the less will get done between meetings, and the longer your board meetings become.

91. No one should ever be surprised at board meetings.

Let board members know when something significant happens with the company – whether positive or negative. Don't let the first time the board hears about the first six-figure account the company landed months after the deal. In a similar vein, if the company is suffering some cash flow issues, inform the board right away even if the next board meeting isn't scheduled for several weeks.

Lesson for entrepreneurs:

Keep great communication with your board. Talk in between board meetings. Reach out to board members with critical issues, as they come up. Don't wait weeks for the board meeting to share big news, whether good or bad. Your board can be a great asset, if you use it right.

92. You aren't a company until you have payroll.

Anything you are doing and not getting paid for is a hobby, so as long as you are working on your idea without compensating yourself or others you are still pre-real company. Companies are made up of people. People are paid.

Lesson for entrepreneurs:

Your first payday for yourself and your team is a milestone. It's the day you have grown from an idea or a hobby to a company.

93. Prime directive in a startup – don't run out of money.

The number one rule of finance is "**cash is king.**" This rule is especially important for entrepreneurs. There are a lot of things you can do without money, including brainstorming and conducting interviews. However, there are also a lot of things you need money to do, such as hiring people and building product. Once you have payroll (which we already know is a milestone for actually being a company) cash becomes particularly important because it is one resource used to keep your team around. Cash fuels your company. Without it, things can quickly start to spiral downhill.

Lesson for entrepreneurs:

Without money you're dead, so don't run out of it. Keep on top of the details, especially understanding cash flows for your business. The more you understand when and how much money is coming in and out, the less likely you are to be blindsided if your checks bounce.

94. If a company succeeds, the entrepreneurs deserve the credit. If a company fails, the investors share the burden with the entrepreneurs.

I think this partially stems from investors' cynical nature. They have to be. Someone needs to look for holes, ask the tough questions, and challenge thinking.

When an investor's portfolio company is acquired and returns an investor's money, it's the entrepreneurs' win. They built the company.

On the flip side, if something doesn't go well, investors take blame. Maybe a company needs to be shut down, or it is sold for a loss on investment. In those cases, investors wonder what more they could have done to help the company succeed. What introductions could have been made, which hard questions weren't asked, which holes were left undiscovered. These situations are great learning opportunities.

Lesson for entrepreneurs:

Investors are your partners. They are on your team and want the team to win. When it comes to the final buzzer and there's a victory, investors won't count up their points and hold their head in glory. They'll give you a high five. When the team loses, investors will look back to their turnovers. Be a team player and recognize investors want you to win.

95. It's not the best company that wins, it is the least fucked up.

Every company has its body odor, its problems. At the end of the day the companies with the least problems succeed.

This advice proved especially helpful when considering my next venture. After spending several years in venture capital, I looked at every company I explored with a critical eye. Each company had some problems. No company was perfect. I needed to figure out, for myself, which problems I could encounter.

Every company has its problems. Problems are inevitable. The quantity and magnitude of those problems are what can kill the company. To throw in another dating analogy, company problems are like individual deal breakers. Most people have a list of deal breakers that can break a relationship before it even begins. Some common ones include: smoking, lying, owning cats. Similarly, certain company characteristics may be deal breakers to a talented individual looking to join a company. Some examples of company deal breakers include: lack of transparency, passive aggression in management, lousy perks, PC-only policy, and dress code.

Whether you're leading a company or not, the first step is figuring out what your company's body odor smells like. Finding the stench is probably going to take more than your nose, though. Spend time with your team, learning about what people like, don't like, and would like to change. Once you have identified your company's issues then you can find the right deodorant to minimize the smell or the right antiperspirant to stop the sweat in the first place.

Lesson for entrepreneurs:

If you're leading the charge, be aware of your company's body odor. The best way to mitigate stench is to sense it and then do something about it (like applying a deodorant). It's better to be honest with yourself and proactive enough to fix the problem before you significantly damage your relationships with your employees, customers, and investors.

If you're looking to join a company, recognize that every company has its problems. Know your deal breakers, but don't get too hung up on finding a perfect, problem-less company. They don't exist.

96. Governance isn't as important as the relationship with the entrepreneur. The working relationship is just as important as the formal relationship between an investor and entrepreneur.

It doesn't matter if an investor is on a board. The relationship with the entrepreneur is far more important than the title of "Board Member." Some entrepreneurs have better relationships and more trust in non-board members, making those non-board members even more influential than the board members.

The formality of investor-entrepreneur relationship isn't reason enough for a good working relationship. Board members aren't always the most influential voices to the entrepreneur. If an investor, not on the board, has a better working relationship with the entrepreneur, you can bet that investor will be more influential to the entrepreneur's decisions. The investor with the better working relationship is going to be the first person the entrepreneur calls.

I witnessed several times when entrepreneurs first turned to non-board members for advice, simply because the entrepreneur trusted those individuals and valued their opinion on the topic at hand more than the opinions of formal board members. Sometimes the formalities of a board do not allow for those special mentors or valuable investors to have a seat in the actual boardroom, but they still have a seat on the entrepreneur's shoulder.

Lesson for entrepreneurs:

Build strong working relationships with your investors regardless of their board member status. Just because someone is on your board, doesn't grant them entitlement to that relationship. If you have a better relationship with a non-board member investor, fine. You can call that investor before board members. (As long as you didn't sign any legal agreements that preclude you from doing so).

Just because an investor or mentor isn't on your company's board doesn't mean it's a relationship not worth fostering. Some of your best advice may come from non-board members. Reach out to and build relationships with your investors regardless of their board roles. If an investor adds value and you learn from your conversations, keep that relationship strong. These relationships may provide tremendous insight and guidance to building a business.

97. VCs...we actually aren't literate anymore. I can't read. I'm a VC.

Enough said.

VCs tend to not read anything more than a few sentences. It takes immense focus for VCs to read through an entire document (not an activity all VCs do). Ask a VC when she/he last read an entire business plan...and don't be surprised if she/he doesn't remember.

Lesson for entrepreneurs:

When sending materials to investors, opt to share an investor deck versus a business plan. Put plenty of colorful graphs and images in your investor deck. Sometimes, the less words the better. Use less text. Let images and pretty graphs tell your story, but make sure to tell the story!

Keep in mind that investors may ask for your business plan and financials as part of their diligence process. If they ask, send it to them. Putting together a business plan and financials will be more beneficial for you as an entrepreneur, than it will be for the investors. Investors want to know that you have thought through all the various aspects of your business – understanding your market, product, competitive landscape, risks, financial needs, people, and so forth. Write the plan, run the numbers, and distil your story into a pitch that clearly shares your company to investors.

98. You put two attorneys in a room and time gets stretched out.

Attorneys like to talk. Attorneys ask a lot of questions. One attorney in a meeting will make it last a bit longer. Two attorneys in a room and you might as well bring plenty of snacks and water to get through the day. Double the attorneys, double the questions.

Lesson for entrepreneurs:

Be patient with the law. It takes time. When patience doesn't work, whine and scream and kick your feet until either one of the attorneys leaves or they get your request completed.

99. Stop trying to boil the ocean.

Focus.

Entrepreneurs face multiple decisions and opportunities every day. Entrepreneurs' jobs are to sort through everything, prioritize, make decisions, and execute. Entrepreneurs trying to boil the ocean will struggle to execute. Trying to do too many things at once is a recipe for disaster.

Before boiling the ocean, find a bay, set sail, conquering one bay at a time until you don't even need the ocean (but you're ready for it!)

Lesson for entrepreneurs:

Focus.

100. Time is the only commodity you can't replace.

Time really is an entrepreneur's most valuable resource. Money can be raised. People can be hired. Time cannot be replaced. An entrepreneur's job becomes all about prioritizing and managing time. There will always be a laundry list of items to do and there will never be enough time in one day to complete them all. If a fortune cookie were to summarize this point it would say "Master the art of spending time wisely and you will meet success."

Lesson for entrepreneurs:

Treat time like your most precious resource, because it is.

On time:

I have heard countless numbers of entrepreneurs (and wantrepreneurs) complain about investors because they take so much time to maintain. It is laughable. Investors take a significant risk when investing in your business and the percent of time you'll end of spending with them is actually far less than everything else you'll spend your time doing.

"I don't have time"

This is the worst excuse for not doing something. We all have time. We all have the same amount of time. 24 hours. 7 days. Yes, Mark Zuckerberg has the same amount of time in a week as you do. So does Barack Obama. I have yet to meet someone with magical powers to actually squeeze more time in a week. It's pretty cut and dry – we all have 24 hours each day. We all **choose** how to spend our time. We choose differently. You **do** have time. Choose wisely how to spend it.

---

101. Not "replying all" is like wearing Velcro shoes. You need to know how to tie your shoes.

Investors do pay attention to the little things, like whether you capitalize names in an email, or even worse, spelling the investors' names wrong (which did happen by the way)! The "reply all" button has become a great tool, but it is commonly misused. Often times, investors will include their colleagues on email responses to entrepreneurs, because ultimately a decision to invest in a company involves getting the VC partnership buy-in. It's a good sign if a VC includes her/his partner and/or junior VCs on an email thread. Don't screw it up by not "replying all" and forcing the VC to continually forward messages and re-copy colleagues to the email thread. Of course, it's not always appropriate to "reply all." Pay attention to the cues and email etiquette.

This advice came out of an investor's mouth after a CEO and Co-Founder didn't reply-all to an email sharing his investor deck with the VC firm. That action entirely inconvenienced the investor, since the investor then needed to forward the deck to the rest of the team (which also creates a time lag in the entire team seeing the materials).

Lesson for entrepreneurs:

When an investor includes colleagues on an email thread, reply all. Once it is not relevant to include certain people on the email thread, take them off. Email etiquette 101.

102. Two startups shouldn't partner up.

Two startups partnering will not get you scale. Such a partnership is not likely going to significantly help you grow your business. Two companies with 10,000 users don't get the large audience needed to scale.

There is an exception to this advice – partnering with other startups is fine, as long as the partnership is not on the critical path to your success. If a good portion of your revenue would come from the partnership with the startup, don't put all your eggs in that basket. Partnering with other startups can also be useful for discovery purposes. For instance, if you are considering launching a new product or service, but first want to partner with someone offering that product/service to see if your customers are interested in that product/service. Partnering with a smaller company early on can also be beneficial for testing out the technology with a small group of people before bringing a large audience through the door. Recognize the purpose and likely outcome from different types of partnerships.

Lesson for entrepreneurs:

Choose partners wisely. Recognize that partnerships with a bunch of startups, early on, are weighted much differently (in VCs' eyes) than partnerships with well-established, large companies. Consider whether the partnership is along your critical path (i.e. it would make up a majority of your revenue) and what purpose the partnership serves. When you can, partner with folks more desperate than you, as this puts you in a position of greater leverage.

103. When faced with a decision between the "right way" and the

"better way," choose the "right way."

When an entrepreneur in our portfolio at RPM Ventures was raising his first equity round for his company (previously he raised convertible notes), one of the VC partners said "there's a 'right way' to do this and a 'better way' to do this" (referring to how to handle putting additional capital into the bridge note before closing the equity round). The "right way" was doing the discount on the bridge note and asking the other investor in the convertible note if he wants to put money in the round. The "better way" was for RPM Ventures to just leak little bits of money into the company's note, with no discount, until the equity round closed. (Investors will leak "little bits of money" in situations like this because with no discount or other sweetener there's no incentive for investors to put money in before the round is fully funded).

Go figure, the "right way" is the right way to go about this situation.

Lesson for entrepreneurs:

When investors ask you to choose between the "right way" and the "better way," choose the "right way."

104. Your company should be bought, not sold.

You're either bought or sold in an acquisition. If you're bought, an acquiring company recognizes the value you created and is paying you for it. If you're sold, you're the driver trying to return money to the shareholders, cash out, or liquidate. You're likely to get a better deal in the former case.

For example, there was a company in our portfolio that was running out of cash and struggling to raise more capital. The company hadn't achieved enough milestones or proven enough traction to make a strong case for an investor to invest more capital. The company was forced to seek potential acquisition opportunities, quickly building strategic relationships. The CEO was trying to sell the company. When an offer was made to acquire the company, the unattractive offer reflected the fact that the company was looking to sell (versus the acquirer looking to buy).

It may seem like a subtle difference, but it really does make an impact. The act of buying demonstrates need and value and will reflect in the acquisition price.

Lesson for entrepreneurs:

Create value in your company so that you can be bought, not sold.

105. If you build a company to get acquired, it likely won't. If you build a company to grow, it may get acquired.

Why are companies acquired? Ultimately, because the acquiring company recognizes value in the acquisition target. That value may be related to team, product, revenue, market penetration, and so forth, or some combination thereof. If getting acquired is your goal in itself, you're not setting yourself up for a real satisfactory journey. The truth of the matter is that most companies aren't acquired for millions or billions of dollars. Though you may read about a few cases of young companies getting acquired before generating revenue, these are fringe cases. And even the companies that are acquired early often set out to build their companies to last before selling.

Lesson for entrepreneurs:

Great entrepreneurs build to grow and sustain, not build to sell. Build your company to be a company, not to be a product for someone else's company. By building to grow a company you are more likely to create value that someone will pay for!

106. The hotter they are, the faster they burn.

The hottest company doesn't win. In fact, sometimes the more popular, famous companies are more destined to fall behind.

Lesson for entrepreneurs:

The hotter your company is, the easier it can catch on fire and burn to a crisp. So don't worry about getting featured on the cover of Forbes or listed as one of the year's "hottest companies." Focus on building your business, solving big problems, and press and success will follow.

107. Whether you win or not, you can always do better.

You may be in a board meeting sharing the great news that you exceed your targets, achieved a record month of sales, and recruited a top-tier VP, and an investor still may say something along the lines of "so what are you going to do better next month so we can hit more sales?"

Lesson for entrepreneurs:

Strive for continuous improvement in business and life. The drive to improve will drive your business to become better and better.

108. Transparency works best for everything.

Transparency in the fundraising process is the only way to build a relationship with investors. Be honest. Be open. Investors have seen enough bullshit that they can also sense it. Your team will also react positively toward great transparency.

Take this example – which CEO would you prefer to work with?

CEO A is incredibly transparent. He has gone so far to share the capitalization table with the entire team, and explained what it means to everyone. He shared his fundraising pitch and updates with the team as well.

CEO B refuses to disclose the value of the company's options or the existing capitalization table with the team.

For me, the decision is obvious (given no other data to make a decision, of course). I want to work for CEO A.

Why does this transparency matter? If employees understand the potential worth of their options and know about the growth trajectory of the company, they are more likely to be motivated to work hard to achieve company goals, than if they are left in the dark. If a CEO isn't transparent about small things, it's less likely that she/he will be honest about other important events with the company (i.e. running out of money, achieving company goals, raising additional capital).

Lesson for entrepreneurs:

Be transparent. It's as simple as that.

109. Make no small plans.

Investors like big thinkers and big market opportunities. Multi-billion dollar market opportunities. Investors invest in big plans. Think big, act big! If you have an ambitious plan and huge market – go for it. Don't skimp when figuring out how much money you need to raise or how many people you need to hire. If you need the resources, ask for them. Don't sell yourself short. Be realistic, but not limiting.

Lesson for entrepreneurs:

Think big! Share your big plans with investors because investors fund big solutions to big problems.

110. Building a company is like riding a subway, not an airplane. There are many stops along the way.

When you ride a train or subway there are several stops where you can get off. Similarly, when building a company there are several departure points along the way. In either case, you have to decide when and where to get off.

For instance, at some point you may get an offer to acquire your company. You can take the offer, negotiate the offer, or reject the offer and stick on the subway. There's always a risk that the next step actually won't be better than the last. Remember when Groupon turned down a $6 billion acquisition offer from Google? Many wondered why Groupon didn't choose that stop to get off and take the offer. Groupon decided to stick on the subway, probably thinking the next steps could be better for the company. Whether or not that was the best decision for the company I'll leave to your own analysis.

Lesson for entrepreneurs:

You will make decision points along the journey of building your company. Whether it's hiring decisions, raising capital, launching new products, or others, you'll lead your company's direction and be part of the decision about which stop to get off.

111. "Startup" starts with "start."

Just start the company! We've all heard that entrepreneur (or more likely, wantrepreneur) talk and talk and talk about starting a company, but never taking any action. Don't be that person. Start it! You'll learn a lot along the way, but the best way to start learning is to start doing!

Lesson for entrepreneurs:

Like Nike always says, "Just Do It!"

8 INSPIRATION

You found a problem
You'd love to solve
You found the people
You want to involve

You sized the market
It's in the billions
You learned to prioritize
Top 3 from the zillions

You have the plan
To win the market
You have the story
And a fundraising target

You built relationships
With mentors and investors
You collected data
From beta testers

You know the customer
Better than you know you
Better now than never
Time to go do

Enjoy the venture!

9 THE AUTHOR

Mary is an entrepreneur. She started her first real business, Iorio's, at age 14, which grew to become a self-sustaining operating business even a decade later. During her time at the University of Michigan, as a full-time student and entrepreneur, Mary started and helped grow several different ventures, from organic cotton apparel to medical devices and clean tech. Also while at the University of Michigan Mary co-founded an internet company, grew her existing business, and built relationships with and learned from successful entrepreneur and investor mentors, all while attending classes. Upon graduating Mary joined RPM Ventures, an early stage venture capital firm investing in internet and software companies. Her experiences working in venture capital provide the inspiration for this book.

Learn more about Mary at her website, www.marylemmer.com.

MARY LEMMER

10 THE LIST

MARY LEMMER

THE PEOPLE

1. People love the idea of being part of building something.
2. Best cultures are deliberately designed and not something you fall into.
3. The difference between a corporate employee and an employee in a startup company is that a corporate employee is more concerned with her/his career, and a startup employee is more concerned with the success of the company.
4. Nothing brings a team together like a common enemy.
5. Investors believe you can do that which you've done in the past.
6. Anybody who is talented is not available.
7. You can tell people, but sometimes you need to show people.
8. If you're a dabbler, you're never successful.
9. A weakness is a strength if you know it's a weakness.
10. Contractors ease you through the gates of hell. I've never seen a successful company built with all contractors.
11. There is no good or bad culture...just the culture you want to build.
12. Somebody who wants to work in a startup already knows it.
13. There is an art of not letting someone say "no" if they're not going to say "yes."
14. Don't put your destiny in the hands of other people.
15. Sometimes your best VP of Sales is someone from Sales Operations.
16. Everyone has his or her own personal obsessive-compulsive disorder (OCD) and it's important to honor it.
17. Entrepreneurs user capital they have to prove they deserve more. Wantrepreneurs complain they don't have enough capital.
18. Entrepreneurs know they have things to figure out and have a framework to do so. Wantrepreneurs think they have it figured out.
19. Entrepreneurs understand that there is little correlation between intellect and achievement. Desire and work ethic matter more.
20. There's no perfect CEO. You just have to be yourself.
21. You want to enter just as well as you exit.
22. Once you hire, they are like cows.
23. The second you stop honoring yourself as CEO is the second you fail as a leader.
24. Investors don't invest in part-time entrepreneurs.
25. Don't give away big titles too soon.
26. You can always give someone more equity later on, but once you

give it you cannot get it back.

27. Successful failure. Every entrepreneur needs to have one.
28. When the Chief Financial Officer (CFO) starts talking about Generally Accepted Accounting Principles (GAAP), you know you have the wrong person.
29. A dog with two owners dies of hunger.
30. If you're doing it right, you should be spending half your time recruiting/building your team.

THE MARKET

31. The best businesses tend to follow the money.
32. Any market under $1 billion is not interesting.
33. The best entrepreneurs are the ones that know their customers better than they know themselves.
34. Focus on one market opportunity.
35. It's great when you build something and you are the customer.
36. You have to go out there and talk to folks.
37. Any attractive market has competition.
38. So you're going to bet your future on someone else's opinion?
39. Great feedback doesn't come from a vacuum.
40. Once you get them on the platform and using it, then you have to tell them why they should be using it, and you can sell them more stuff.
41. You cannot let your customer define your business model.
42. We can all sell stuff to our friends. Go out and sell to someone you don't know.
43. If you don't know what the customer is looking for how can you build them something?
44. If you're going to burn a market, burn one that no one gives a shit about.
45. The roadside is littered with companies that tried to sell to the small and medium business (SMB) market.
46. You don't need a beta product to demonstrate customer demand. And a survey isn't going to cut it.

THE MODEL

47. All the factors of value proposition drive business model.
48. Track your experiments. Track results.
49. Know your model – if you put $X in, you will get how much out?

50. SaaS is not a buzzword. It's a way of doing business.
51. Show me a business, not a product.
52. Facebook "likes" don't convert to revenue.
53. If you pivot more than once you're spinning in a circle.

THE PRODUCT

54. Create a sticky widget.
55. That time at the keyboard becomes so much more productive when it's backed by user-driven design. Now you know why you're coding.
56. If it has a plug it's not getting funded.
57. There are no new ideas. It's all in the execution.
58. It's not always the best product that wins. It's the best distribution.
59. Create an illusion of bigness.
60. Sell scarcity.
61. Owning inventory is so 1990s.

THE FUNDRAISE

62. The best pitches are not pitches. They are conversations.
63. You have to build a crescendo into fundraising. Build your story.
64. For everything you say in an elevator pitch, there should be some reason you're putting it there.
65. If you screw up your pitch, don't say anything at the end. Most likely your audience won't notice.
66. If I don't get it, it's your fault, not mine.
67. A deck has to stand alone without a story because it will circulate throughout the firm.
68. If I go like this it means go faster.
69. "I think" isn't good enough. You should "know."
70. You can lie with statistics, but you can't deny the facts.
71. What are the three most important things the company must do to prove you can tackle the market?
72. A business plan is a static document and there's no such thing as a static startup.
73. Over half of fundraising is timing. (Finding a partner when they have bandwidth, timing for partner's fund, etc.)
74. We don't sign NDAs because it is for the entrepreneurs' protection.
75. We don't invest unless we can add value.

76. We won't invest in a company that we wouldn't want to work in as entrepreneurs.
77. We don't believe in overcapitalizing companies. We believe in capitalizing them enough, and holding money in reserve.
78. There is no science for valuing companies. There are tools.
79. Investors care about post-money.
80. Right way to get a term sheet done: start by agreeing you want to do the deal. Wrong way: start by negotiating details.
81. Don't agree to anything until deal is closed.
82. Money is a resource for entrepreneurs, but time is more precious. The math: money will not solve all your problems. To think so is folly.

THE LIFE

83. If it were easy everybody would be doing it.
84. Once you take investor money you have a responsibility to them more than just their money.
85. Sometimes luck is your best ally.
86. Don't count your chickens before they hatch.
87. Don't sign leases for more than two years.
88. The worst way to negotiate is to make an assumption about how people are going to negotiate.
89. Expectations are a source of disappointment.
90. So many entrepreneurs think board meetings are mystical, and they make a big deal of them. All the real work is done behind the scenes. Board meetings are actually really boring.
91. No one should ever be surprised at board meetings.
92. You aren't a company until you have payroll.
93. Prime directive in a startup – don't run out of money.
94. If a company succeeds, the entrepreneurs deserve the credit. If a company fails, the investors share the burden with the entrepreneurs.
95. It's not the best company that wins, it is the least fucked up.
96. Governance isn't as important as relationship with entrepreneur. The working relationship is just as important as the formal relationship between an investor and entrepreneur.
97. VCs...we actually aren't literate anymore. I can't read. I'm a VC.
98. You put two attorneys in a room and time gets stretched out.
99. Stop trying to boil the ocean.
100. Time is the only commodity you can't replace.
101. Not "replying all" is like wearing Velcro shoes. Need to know how

to tie your shoes.

102.Two startups shouldn't partner up.

103.When faced with a decision between the "right way" and the "better way," choose the "right way."

104.Your company should be bought, not sold.

105.If you build a company to get acquired, it likely won't. If you build a company to grow, it may get acquired.

106.The hotter they are, the faster they burn.

107.Whether you win or not, you can always do better.

108.Transparency works best for everything.

109.Make no small plans.

110.Building a company is like riding a subway, not an airplane. There are many stops along the way.

111."Startup" starts with "start."

MARY LEMMER